WELCOME TO
Mount Merry College

The gates of learning: the gates of Mount Merry.

PHOTO BUG

WELCOME TO
Mount Merry College

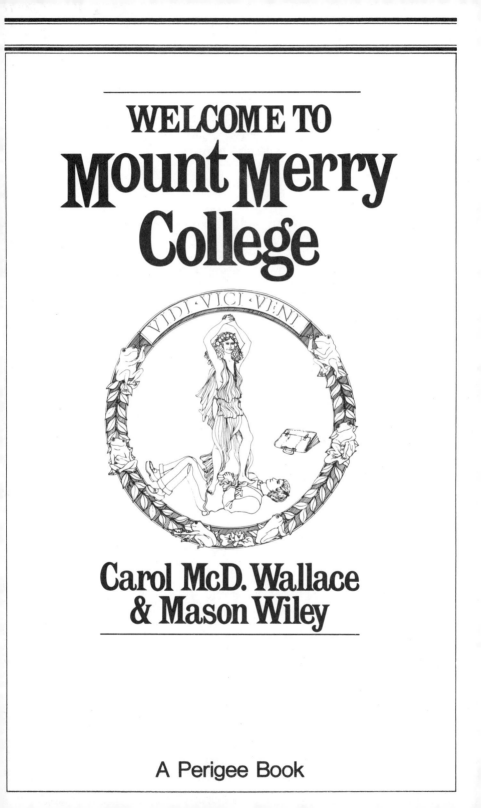

VIDI · VICI · VENI

Carol McD. Wallace
& Mason Wiley

A Perigee Book

Perigee Books
are published by
G. P. Putnam's Sons
200 Madison Avenue
New York, New York 10016

Library of Congress Cataloging in Publication Data
Wallace, Carol, date.
  Welcome to Mount Merry.

  "A Perigee book."
  I. Wiley, Mason.   II. Title.
PS3573.A42563W4   813'.54   81-15409
ISBN 0-399-50615-2   AACR2

Interior design by Bernard Schleifer
Logo design by Iris Bass

First Perigee printing, 1982

Printed in the United States of America

One of Mount Merry's friendly faces.

HOW TO USE THIS CATALOG

PLEASE EXAMINE THE table of contents on page 7. Find the topic you want to read about. Draw a straight line with your finger across the page (don't use a pencil because someone else might read this after you) and find what page it's on. Turn the pages, and start reading.

PHOTO BUG

CONTENTS

PHOTO BUG

Students sharing the joys of learning are a common sight on Mount Merry's campus.

WHY MOUNT MERRY?

WHY SHOULD MOUNT MERRY BE the place for you? Mount Merry is a relatively small, coeducational, residential, and not very demanding college located on a compact campus in Waterbury, Connecticut. That's all true. But there's so much more to Mount Merry: in the words of one distinguished graduate, Orville Plunkett, "When you've said Mount Merry, you've said a mouthful!"

GOALS

Mount Merry is a serious institution, dedicated to the education of our students and to the fulfillment of certain missions. It is the purpose of the college to foster, nurture, promote, endorse, and nourish the development of each totally unique individual's best personal self. At Mount Merry, through the search for truth with knowledge and responsibility, students become truly integrated persons. This process occurs as students participate in the Mount Merry experience, always bearing in mind the following specific goals of the college:

1. To ascertain that Mount Merry students achieve a certain level of academic competence. Life in the United States today is demanding in the extreme; it is essential that, to become their best integrated personal selves, students be able to go to extremes as well, including with each other;

2. To expose students to some of the more important aspects—political, social, artistic, scientific, economic, cultural, inter- and intrapersonal (students usually pick one)—of Western society to date;

3. To guarantee that, when students forsake the ever-welcoming shelter of Mount Merry's compact campus, they will be enabled, as their best integrated personal individual selves, to make a significant, valid contribution to modern society by maintaining regular gainful employment at least at the minimum wage;

4. To encourage students to be strong, healthy physical specimens, trained and fit and able to contribute in a healthy, robust, physical way to today's world;

5. To provide a challenging but encouraging academic experience that will provoke curiosity while stimulating confidence, above all ensuring that students know a little bit about some things and feel capable of learning a little bit more if they ever need to;

6. To open new vistas.

THE FACULTY

The faculty at Mount Merry enjoys a number of unique advantages, which in turn benefit the students. They are unilaterally committed to undergraduate education—to a Mount Merry professor, the most fun and the greatest challenge in life is teaching a Mount Merry student. You will enjoy learning at Mount Merry because the faculty is learning along with you.

Mount Merry professors are true professionals, too. More than half of them hold or share college degrees. Best of all is Mount Merry's famous "no-tenure" policy. Since faculty members are never granted tenure, they are under no obligation to "publish or perish," nor need they waste their time on research. What's more, the no-tenure policy assures a stimulating mix of old and well-beloved professors steeped in Mount Merry traditions and ways, and a variety of young professors eager to experiment with new teaching methods and theories.

Because of the relatively small size of Mount Merry, you'll find that it's easy to become friendly with the faculty. Class attendance is low, averaging around fifteen, and the student-faculty ratio is 33:1. Most faculty members live on campus, in or near the same facilities as the students. You'll find them everywhere—at breakfast, on the playing field, in the Padded Cell (the student "hangout"), in the Hair Care Center. The intercourse between students and faculty is one of the best things about Mount Merry.

THE STUDENTS

Mount Merry is the third oldest coeducational institution of higher learning in Waterbury, and this unique advantage makes it attractive to a considerable variety of students, male and female. Students come to Mount Merry from at least a dozen states and several foreign countries, including Canada. In 1974, a French student spent a semester at Mount Merry, truly contributing to the international flair and aura of the school. The student attrition/retention rate at Mount Merry is extraordinary; of the 529 students matriculating in 1978, 32 percent finished one year, 12 percent finished two years, and 18 percent finished five or more years at Mount Merry.

Mount Merry is proud of her graduates and other students. An average of two dozen each year go on to further education in such institutions as driving school, secretarial school, and bartender's school. Counted among its recent graduates are: Cissy Patsy, Special Assistant for Physical Affairs to State Assemblyman Carmine Lobrano; Running-Squirrel-Without-a-Tail, poet laureate of the Southwestern Fairfield County chapter of the Sioux Nation; St. John St. Albert, superior partner in the decorating firm of All Saints (specializing in ecclesiastical decor); and Dr. Enid Gall, Chief of Surgery at the Hospital for Cosmetic Veterinary Surgery in Crawfordsville, Indiana. Furthermore, Mount Merrians are distinguishing themselves in small ways all over the nation as professionals, homemakers, community leaders, and, occasionally, scholars—and even from time to time as all four. When you join the student body of Mount Merry, you'll find you're inheriting a rich tradition and joining a broad group of distinguished, fun-loving, totally unique individuals with whom you'll have in common four years of your life that you will remember.

THE WATERBURY ADVANTAGE

Mount Merry's location in downtown Waterbury is considered by some to be the school's greatest advantage. Proximity to some of Connecticut's most picturesque towns and to convenient Interstate 84 (which connects Danbury with New Britain), are only two of the features Waterbury offers. The majestic Naugatuck River runs right through town, and the even more majestic Connecticut River is only a short drive away. Best of all, downtown Waterbury offers a real "slice of life" situation. The 79¢ beers at Benny's Grill are a popular facet of Waterbury's culture.

A unique blend of activities makes life on the Mount Merry campus always interesting. Whether attending hootenanny sessions in the residence halls or enjoying the clean and convenient bathroom facilities or sharing a moment of togetherness with your several roommates, you'll find a special feeling at Mount Merry. Social opportunities range from the annual formal sponsored by the Ranology Center to popular frat parties, and the faculty often joins in. Men and women get along just fine at Mount Merry; they often meet socially as well as in class. Or they may be drawn together by some of the cultural opportunities in Waterbury or on campus. Waterbury's movie theater sometimes shows the finest in family entertainment, while the campus cinema shows a number of "art" films each year. Visitors come to Mount Merry to perform for the students and everybody has fun. Recent guests have included Steve Lawrence and Eydie Gorme (1976), Lawrence Welk (1977), Liberace (1978), Steve Lawrence and Eydie Gorme (1979) and Marie Osmond (1980). This roster of exciting entertainers is often complemented by thought-provoking writers and poets such as G. Gordon Liddy and Suzanne Somers.

Naturally the athletic focus of Mount Merry plays a large part in its appeal to prospective students. The modern, up-to-date facilities include a gym and lockers (with three showers), and a low-maintenance playing field. Mount Merry students participate actively in sports at all levels, making athletics an enticing part of the dynamic Mount Merry experience.

The four-year physical education requirement guarantees that everyone at Mount Merry enjoys sports.

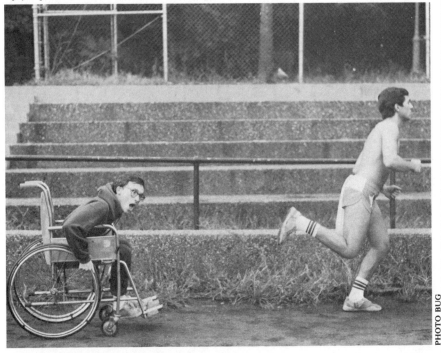

PHOTO BUG

CHAPLAIN'S ESSAY

STEEPED IN TRADITION, Mount Merry College is a community that is proud of its uniquely rich heritage. Founded in 1894 as a Catholic Seminary by Garland Rooney, a leading civic leader who amassed a considerable fortune in the firearms industry, Mount Merry began its glorious career in the then thriving and expanding city of Waterbury, Connecticut, where it remains today. Rooney founded the school in the memory of his beloved late son, Fauntleroy, a precocious child with a keen interest in frogs who passed away in the lily pond in front of what is now the administrative building. To honor Fauntleroy's predilection for frogs, Rooney chose the noble frog as the school mascot and the colors green and brown—green representing "the frog" and brown "the earth on which it lives"—as the school colors.

In 1896, two years after its establishment, Mount Merry began admitting undergraduate students to meet the growing awareness of the importance of the undergraduate college in American life as well as to counterbalance the drop in graduate applications to the Seminary. The Seminary was dissolved shortly thereafter.

The neighboring Carrie Nation Temperance College for Women was founded in 1919 by three maiden sisters, Miss Hildegarde, Miss Agnes, and Miss Gertrude Klumpp. Based on the principles of "imparting physical, moral, and spiritual education to its students so that they may be useful and sober members of society," the college was efficiently administered by the Klumpps for most of their lengthy lives and funded by their well-managed portfolio of stocks in household paper products and grooming aids. The splendidly designed Carrie Nation campus was distinguished by the tall brick wall that separated it from Mount Merry's campus.

In 1943, I stepped in as chaplain when it was discovered that the previous chaplain had died the year before. Mrs. Mildred Maim, the school secretary at Carrie Nation, assumed the role of headmistress there in 1954 when the last of the Klumpp sisters was declared legally senile. Mrs. Maim soon began to work with me in the gratifying act of bringing our two academic bodies into closer contact and interaction.

In 1975, Mrs. Maim and I decided to merge the venerable Mount Merry with the affluent Carrie Nation. Mount Merry's Board of Trustees applauded the action for its scholarly intent and financial wisdom. The Board of Directors of Carrie Nation instantaneously granted Mrs. Maim an honorary nonregulatory position in deference to her long years of service and, after a four-year search for a new headmistress, appointed Dr. Vonetta Fitzcox, former president of the Babe Didrikson College of Physical Culture, to the office of Chancellor Under the Chaplain. Mrs. Maim currently divides her time between announcing the annual Maim Scholars at commencement and residing in her condominium in Miami Beach.

Grasping fully what Shakespeare meant when he wrote, "There's nothing new under the sun," we at Mount Merry realize that so-called "new approaches" to education are utter nonsense, that nothing has replaced the time-honored methods of discipline and memorization that have been practiced by students here for almost a century and will continue unchanged for centuries more.

DR. REGINALD KAISER
College Chaplain

CHANCELLOR'S ESSAY

MOUNT MERRY is a community on the go. We at Mount Merry don't rest on our laurels or dwell on the past—we look ahead, and it's this dynamic progressiveness in education that makes Mount Merry such an exciting place to be today.

When I accepted this post in 1979, I made a commitment to Mount Merry, to the students here, and to myself, that I would do everything possible to keep Mount Merry at the vanguard of the new directions in modern higher education. I set as my goal the task of making this college a national byword in academic excellence and invention. I believe that students today want "something else" from college rather than just their schoolwork, and at Mount Merry, they get it. Our plan of study is concentrated on the student as a whole person, and every aspect of life, academic or non, is geared toward creating that whole person as I envision him or her.

PHOTO BUG

When I arrived at Mount Merry, I saw that students needed a flexibility in the scholastic program to help them achieve the aims they had set for themselves. Believing that education should be a highway to knowledge and not a dead-end road, I initiated a number of innovations in the course of study that students have benefited from. The Pass/Fail Option® has relieved students from the pressure of going to class. The short Winter term courses have offered students opportunities to take interesting, offbeat courses and to satisfy required courses quickly. The interdisciplinary courses give students a chance to study nonacademic but practical subjects that will actually have some bearing on their later lives.

In short, I have introduced these new features to show students that Mount Merry is not afraid to change with the times. We ask you to join us in the ongoing academic adventure here at Mount Merry. As we look for new ways to learn and study, we'd like you to be a part of our scholastic experiment. As the Klumpp sisters maintained so forcefully years ago, "Resoluteness of purpose always gets results," and I'm sure that you, too, can get what you want here at our happy, compact campus.

MS. VONETTA FITZCOX, PH.D
College Chancellor

"I have been very happy with my teachers so far. If you need help, they always tell you where their office is."

ROSCOE KURTIS JENKINS
East New York, NY

"Math was a lot harder than I thought it was going to be."

KIMBERLY BERKOWITZ
Scarsdale, NY

"I chose Mount Merry because it is small and the campus is compact."

TINA NG
Los Angeles, CA

"At first I thought Waterbury was a cultural wasteland, but I gave it a chance."

PETER VAN NESS (currently on LOAF)
Seymour, CT

"My younger brothers told me about Mount Merry, and it turned out to be everything they promised."

RALPH OXENWALD, JR.
Blue Balls, PA

"As a pre-Ranology student, I judiciously evaluated the course offerings of numerous illustrious institutions. In my carefully estimated opinion, Mount Merry is unparalleled in this specific field."

BUCKY GOOBER
Lizard Lick, NC

"The one thing I like about Mount Merry, they really know how to par-tee!"

TOWNSEND "BUD" WEISER
Charlottesville, VA

"I was attracted to Mount Merry by the female coaching staff. They're always willing to lend you a hand."

ALICE B. GUDUNOV
Bath, ME

"While a lot of students really get into the Greek life, you don't have to feel left out if you're not Greek. Everybody here likes to get together and have fun, whether they're having a beer at the Padded Cell or taking the bus to the Danbury airport."

ARISTOTLE LALAOUNIS
Long Island City, NY

"For someone who wants to meet members of the opposite sex, Mount Merry is a good enough place to start."

ANGELINA DELL FUNICELLO
Narrowsburg, NJ

"At Mount Merry, it becomes abundantly clear that your teachers are all too human, just like you."

MICHAEL GREEN
Manhattan, NY

"There are so many opportunities to get involved at Mount Merry, sometimes it seems as if no one is taking advantage of them."

TAMMY SIMPLET
Emporia, KS

"Once you tell people you go to Mount Merry, you find their perception of you changes."

RUFUS KALE
Exeter, NH

"The rapport with nearby male schools is great. They're always happy to see Mount Merry girls."

HAPPY McCOLL
Moorestown, NJ

"I really like the class discussions. The teachers are really open and they'll talk about anything you want."

HORACE SUMP
Needham, MA

"The grading system lets you work at your own level, without any pressure, knowing that you'll do OK."

DORIS KLEGELHOFFER
Fall River, MA

"Other schools said they had a good curriculum, but with Mount Merry, you knew exactly what you're getting into."

LOU GORELIK
Teaneck, NJ

"A good thing about Mount Merry is that you have plenty of free time. I have a job in Waterbury. I'm a bouncer in a bar and that's pretty interesting. It pays alright. I met some nice people."

RUDY DAKINS
Waterbury, CT

CALENDAR

August 1 (Sun.)	Tuition deadline. No student admitted if check is not received and cleared by this date
August 15–29 (Sun.–Wed.)	English Training Camp for English Majors
August 30 (Thurs.)	New Student Orientation
August 31 (Fri.)	Old Student Re-Orientation
Sept. 1–3 (Sat.–Mon.)	Labor Day Holiday
Sept. 4 (Tues.)	Registration of all former Mount Merry students, readmitted or otherwise. Courses on a first-come, first-served basis
Sept. 5 (Wed.)	Registration of unsuspecting freshmen
Sept. 6 (Thurs.)	Sunrise Mass and Opening Convocation Fall term classes begin, 8:00 A.M.
Sept. 20 (Thurs.)	Late Registration for students who did not have the good sense to register earlier. Late registration fees payable in cash (used $10 and $20 bills only, in non-consecutive serial numbers) to School Comptroller Izzy A. Shyster
Oct. 1 (Mon.)	Last date to change a course
Oct. 8 (Mon.)	Really last date to change a course
Oct. 15 (Mon.)	Penalty date for changing a course. Students answer to Holy Office
Oct. 20 (Fri.)	Midterm examinations begin
Oct. 27 (Fri.)	Midterm examinations end
Oct. 28 (Sat.)	Homecoming Weekend
Nov. 8 (Fri.)	Last day student can officially withdraw from college without failing grades on permanent record that will haunt you for the rest of your life
Nov. 27 (Thurs.)	Thanksgiving
Nov. 28 (Fri.)	Last day of classes
Dec. 1 (Mon.)	Reading Period
Dec. 15 (Mon.)	Final examinations begin

PHOTO BUG

A biology experiment.

Dec. 20 (Fri.)	Sybarite Festival (exams suspended)
Dec. 21 (Sat.)	Final exams resume
Dec. 23 (Tues.)	Final examinations end
Dec. 24 (Wed.)	Christmas vacation begins
Jan. 2 (Fri.)	Winter term classes begin
Jan. 5 (Mon.)	Fall term final grades posted
Jan. 6 (Tues.)	Last day to drop a Fall term course; Contention Period
Jan. 16 (Fri.)	Winter term classes end
Jan. 19 (Mon.)	Winter term reading period
Feb. 3 (Mon.)	Winter term examinations begin
Feb. 14 (Fri.)	Winter term examinations end
Feb. 17 (Mon.)	Spring term classes begin
Feb. 26–27 (Tues.–Wed.)	Mardi Gras/Ash Wednesday Celebration

March 5–6 (Tues.–Wed.)	Parents' Weekend
March 15 (Mon.)	Midterm examinations begin
March 20 (Fri.)	Midterm examinations end
April 4 (Thurs.)	Maundy Thursday (Classes suspended)
April 5 (Fri.)	Good Friday (Classes suspended)
April 6 (Sat.)	Holy Saturday (Classes suspended)
April 7 (Sun.)	Easter Sunday (Classes suspended)
April 8 (Mon.)	Students drunk over weekend suspended
April 21 (Wed.)	Fauntleroy Day
May 7 (Fri.)	Last day of classes
May 10 (Mon.)	Reading Period
May 27 (Mon.)	Memorial Day
June 8 (Fri.)	Final examinations end
June 11 (Mon.)	Spring term final grades posted
June 12 (Tues.)	Contention Period and final day to drop a Spring term course
June 13 (Wed.)	Announcement of candidates for graduation
June 14 (Thurs.)	Contention Period
June 15 (Fri.)	Commencement warm-ups
June 16 (Sat.)	Commencement exercises
June 17 (Sun.)	Dormitory rates change for summer

NOTE: Mount Merry reserves the right to change the calendar arbitrarily and at will, or to cancel the school year altogether.

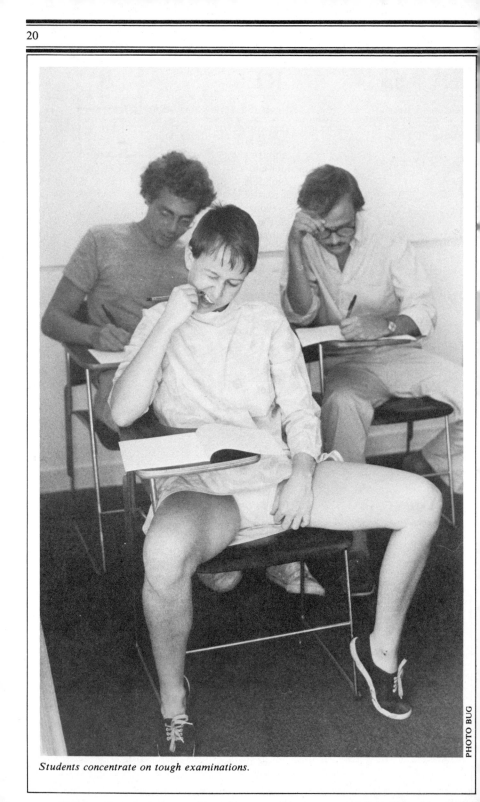

PHOTO BUG

Students concentrate on tough examinations.

RULES AND REGULATIONS

MOUNT MERRY COLLEGE ASSUMES that students come to the college for a serious purpose and expects them to be responsible individuals who demand of themselves high standards of self-discipline and commitment to education, as demonstrated in academic activities and personal conduct and appearance alike. Disappointments in this regard have been rare. The rules which follow are based on a strict ethic of purity and morality believed to be an integral part of the Mount Merry education. They were drawn up in 1975 by Rev. Moses Savonarola, on the occasion of the merger of the all-male Mount Merry College with the female Carrie Nation Temperance College, in an effort to retain the sterling character of each institution as it existed.

The keystone of all rules and regulations at Mount Merry is the Honor Pledge:

> The most important principle at Mount Merry is the three-way principle of honesty, integrity, and morality in academic and nonacademic life. Trespasses against this standard represent trespasses against the spirit of the college and potential harm to the individual as a vessel for wisdom and growth.

THE RULES

At Mount Merry, the following kinds of behavior are considered to be infractions of the Honor Pledge:

1. Cheating, plagiarism, giving false information, and exaggerating to members of the college community;
2. Forgery or other falsification of report cards, ID cards, meal tickets, or advisers' signatures on registration cards;
3. Obstruction or disruption of teaching, administration, or physical education functions or authorized activities on campus;
4. Physical or verbal abuse of any person including self, or of college-owned or controlled property;
5. Theft or concealment of property of members of the Mount Merry community or campus visitors;
6. Unauthorized entry or use of college facilities, or improper use of keys, WATS line, maintenance vehicles or kitchen equipment;
7. Use or misuse of dangerous drugs as defined by applicable law or prevailing cultural opinion;
8. Disorderly, lewd, indecent, or obscene conduct or expression in dormitories and locker rooms, on campus or college-controlled property, or at college-sponsored events all over the world;
9. All sexual relations outside the bonds of marriage;
10. Helping other Mount Merry students to fulfill their responsibilities under this code.

THE HOLY OFFICE

The Holy Office is the disciplinary arm of the college. Composed of four members of the faculty and administration, it carries out its functions in strictest secrecy, in order to guarantee the anonymity of the offender and the members of the office themselves.

To further insure that the identity of each Holy Officer remain unknown, all meetings take place in the catacombs of the chapel and each officer wears a monk's habit with the cowl pulled over his face.

The Student Government Board, when it determines that a case requires punitive measures, leaves the choice and execution of the chastisement to the Holy Office. The particulars of each offense are left in an envelope in the hollowed-out trunk of a tree on campus, following which the Holy Office takes matters into its own hands. When no cases come before them, the ever-ready Holy Office conducts drills in order to hone their techniques, with members alternating in the role of offender.

In addition to its disciplinary function, the Holy Office maintains a categorical collection of medieval torture devices in prime working order.

STUDENT GOVERNMENT

The college believes that the individual acquires an appreciation of individual responsibility when he is called upon to govern himself. To this end, the Student Government Board has been structured to allow each individual to discover for himself the limits of his own responsibilities.

Every spring three students are elected to the Student Government Board, which handles all disciplinary problems and needs within the student community. The magnitude of these concerns may range from major violations of the rules to requests to drink a beer. In the event that the board deems that the seriousness of the offense warrants severe disciplinary action, they may turn the offender over to the Holy Office. It is to the credit of the Student Government Board (and the student body in general) that, over the past five years, the board has not found it necessary to consign a single case to the Holy Office.

ALCOHOLIC BEVERAGES

Students may not possess or use alcoholic beverages on the Mount Merry campus. Exceptions to this rule will be made only if written permission is obtained from the Student Government Board FOR EACH OCCASION and if adequate provisions are made by the petitioner for the government board itself. Any student becoming intoxicated and acting in a manner that is detrimental to his or her good name or that of the college will be subject to increased popularity.

STANDARDS OF DRESS AND GROOMING

The maintenance of high standards of personal appearance and hygiene is essential to the preservation of an atmosphere that encourages academic pursuit and devotion. Continuing registration at Mount Merry constitutes an affirmative consent to abide thereby.

General: The attire and grooming of both men and women should always be neat and clean. Students are expected to take showers daily and to clean their nails and behind their ears on a regular basis. Lace-up shoes are required in all buildings and public areas of the campus with the exception of the sleeping areas of the residence halls. Shorts are acceptable wear only in living and athletic areas and have no business in the classroom. So-called "grubby" attire (black sneakers, torn jeans, wraparound sunglasses, and sleeveless black T-shirts adorned with safety pins) may be worn only in the immediate living areas of the residence hall, and is considered distasteful in the dining hall.

Men: Beards and long or bushy sideburns are not acceptable. Mustaches are not encouraged, but if worn should be trimmed below the nostrils. Hair must be combed and styled so that it does not cover the ears or the shirt collar. Slacks, ties, sports coats or blazers, suits, and leisure suits are all acceptable menswear for attendance at classes. Jeans and tank tops are forbidden and jump suits regarded with suspicion.

Women: Body hair is not considered attractive or conducive to learning. Mustaches are not encouraged, but if worn should be trimmed below the nostrils. Although hairstyle is up to the individual student's discretion, the administration recommends such neat, attractive styles as the beehive or the flip, with a scarf tied under the chin for informal activities. Acceptable women's wear for attendance at classes includes dresses, shifts, skirts and blouses, sweaters and slacks, pedal pushers or culottes, or modest pantsuits (not including jeans). T-shirts, if worn, must not bear obscene legends and must fit loosely over foundation garments. Formal wear may be either long or short but does not include low-cut necklines or strapless gowns. Halter tops and bare midriffs are not considered appropriate for academic or dining situations inasmuch as professors find them distracting or unappetizing.

PROHIBITIONS

Specifically prohibited from the dormitories are: firearms and explosives, solicitation or offering of services not sanctioned by the college, waterbeds and lava lamps, nuclear materials, and gasoline-powered vehicles (except automobiles).

It should be noted that the college discourages the use of automobiles by students. Because of the compact nature of the campus and its situation in the center of Waterbury, there is little need for students to keep cars in their possession, especially when the pleasant and healthful aspects of walking are considered. Students with satisfactory academic and social standing may, if they insist, keep automobiles, provided that they are registered with School Comptroller Izzy A. Shyster. Students on scholarship may not possess, operate, nor ride in motor vehicles.

The hushed atmosphere of the library fosters an exchange of ideas.

NO FOOD OR DRINK ALLOWED IN READING ROOMS EATING & SMOKING IN LOUNGE; SMOKING ONLY IN ROOM 404

PHOTO BUG

PHOTO BUG

Students on the work-study program.

CURRICULUM

MOUNT MERRY COLLEGE CONFERS two degrees only, the Bachelor of Science (for Ranology students) and Bachelor of Arts (for everyone else). Mount Merry assumes that a student who has elected to enroll must be prepared for certain academic compromises and realizes that earning the degree may entail a significant lowering of standards. Mount Merry requires that the holder of her degree have adequate knowledge of reading and arithmetic and that he be aware of the role of Mount Merry in the history of the world. Each student is urged to plan his academic program in light of his particular abilities and limitations. It is also strongly suggested that the student bear in mind the requirements for graduation.

RESIDENCE
Degree candidates must be students in good standing who have resided on the Mount Merry campus for at least four years, or have paid the equivalent in dorm fees.

PROGRAM PLANNING
In planning their programs, freshmen refer occasionally to their assigned faculty advisers, frequently to their resident student advisers, and constantly to upper-class scuttlebutt. Conferences for freshmen are scheduled with their faculty advisers four times a year. During orientation a student participates in a special conference in which the adviser counsels him at length about his program. At the end of the conference, the adviser will wake the student to give him his registration card, without which he is ineligible to register at the scheduled time. Students attempting to register without their registration cards will have to answer to the Holy Office and will be forced to attend Late Registration, which is not a pretty sight.

Conferences also occur after midterm warnings are distributed in Fall and Spring semesters. The traditional Renewed Purpose Pledge is administered at this time, and students and faculty renegotiate their work-for-credit agreements to include lawn mowing or snow shoveling as dictated by the seasons. The final conference takes place at year's end. Students reluctant to return to Mount Merry are turned over to Prof. Norman Bates for counseling.

COURSE LOAD AND SELECTION
In order to satisfy requirements for graduation, students must complete nineteen academic units during their stay (however long) at Mount Merry. Each one-semester course counts as one unit; Winter term courses, as two. While some students elect to take four courses per semester, many choose to take advantage of the double-point Winter term courses and satisfy all requirements for graduation—except residency—in those sessions. In an effort to achieve the semblance of a liberal education, Mount Merry has insisted on the following distribution requirements. Students may choose one from column A or one from Column B, in each category.

Column A	Column B
Theology and religion	Adequate confession and significant acts of contrition (Episcopalians may write a check)
Laboratory science	Results from any science experiment performed during previous schooling
English or speech	Successful recitation or writing from memory of Joyce Kilmer's "Trees"
Art or music	"Perceptive" evaluation (or purchase) of one of Frank Lloyd Kovalchick's art works

All students are also required to take Elementary Frog Studies and History of Mount Merry College. Owing to its origins as a religious institution, Mount Merry demands at least one credit of extracurricular religious activity, consisting of regular attendance at chapel or parish coffee hour.

PHYSICAL EDUCATION

Upon her promotion to the post of chancellor, Dr. Fitzcox, working hand in hand with Co-chairperson (female) of the Physical Education Department, Mary Dyche, implemented Mount Merry's radical physical education program in an attempt to elevate physical education to physical erudition. This means four years of gym.

TRANSFER CREDITS

Students may present courses previously completed with a passing grade or better from any college that is—or is rumored to be—regionally accredited. Upon payment of a fee equal to tuition for each course, credit will be applied to the student's transcript. It is possible (and encouraged) to satisfy all requirements for the major at other institutions, although the residency requirement must be fulfilled at Mount Merry. Students should be reminded that the administration is well aware that two of the college's required courses—History of Mount Merry and Elementary Frog Studies—are not offered elsewhere, and attempts to transfer credit will be severely rebuffed.

It should be noted that other colleges are highly reluctant to accept Mount Merry credits for transfer.

SUMMER STUDY

Summer vacation provides excellent opportunities for a variety of educational experiences which give added significance to the formal studies of the college curriculum. Many students wish to take courses during Summer session at Mount Merry, and are regularly disappointed, when they arrive, to find the college closed. However, many opportunities for accumulating credit during the summer months do exist. Under the supervision of the Director of Career Counseling, Arnold Botcher, students may earn credit toward their degrees via profitable occupations during the summer months in such fields as busing tables, pumping gas, flipping hamburgers, or bumming across country.

EARLY GRADUATION

Students wishing to be considered for early graduation should confer with School Comptroller Izzy A. Shyster. The usual course of study requires four years, but other arrangements can usually be negotiated.

Human Development students explore themselves and each other.

PHOTO BUG

In the midst of registration hubbub, Kingston Mildew awaits excited history students.

ACADEMIC REGULATIONS

REGISTRATION

ALL STUDENTS ATTENDING CLASSES who expect to study at Mount Merry must register for courses. Continuing students who expect to be enrolled in the following term should register in April for September and December for January, or vice versa. Schedule forms and registration materials are found in heaps in the gym the night before registration. Failure to file with the requisite forms may result in steep fines, and late registration is penalized at $35.00 per hour.

Mount Merry attempts to keep class size manageable, and thus limits course enrollment in most cases. Courses are assigned on a first come, first served basis, so students should bear third- and fourth-choice courses in mind when registering. To insure that each returning student is guaranteed at least one course of his choice during his career at Mount Merry, he is given the opportunity to file a pre-registration request for a single course preference at the beginning of sophomore year. Every effort is made to provide the student with his preferred course during his stay at Mount Merry. Students should keep in mind that, after all, the registrar's office is only human and she cannot honor *every* student's request.

CHANGING COURSES

Choice of courses should not be rashly undertaken, and all selections submitted to the registrar will be considered final. However, students who demonstrate compelling need to change a course may petition via heart-wrenching lamentation, and candidates successful in moving the registrar to tears will have their requests granted. (It should be noted that the registrar regards with extreme skepticism tales of moribund relatives, and death certificates should be available upon request in connection with such cases.)

EXEMPTION

Since Mount Merry wishes to enable every student to advance at a rate commensurate with his ability and ambition, students who believe they are competent in a degree-required course and wish to be exempted from it should indicate this to the professor. The instructor may elect to administer a placement test or simply to take the student at his word. A student who demonstrates unusual ability on the placement test may be exempted from the course, given credit, and made eligible for cash prizes chosen by a random drawing.

If a student considers himself sufficiently talented or experienced in one of the activities that meet the aims of the extracurricular physical education requirement, he must demonstrate his proficiency in a letter (of more than one hundred words) to either Mr. Steve E. Dore or Professor Dyche. Illustrations will not be accepted.

CHOOSING A MAJOR

By the end of sophomore year all students must choose a major of concentration. Although the administration recognizes than an imaginative or iconoclastic spirit can be an advantage in academics, Mount Merry does offer twenty-seven majors, and students should be able to find one that appeals to them. Indecisive sophomores may find it helpful to correlate their postgraduate career ambitions with their undergraduate studies (e.g., businessman/business, game show host/mass communications).

TRANSCRIPT

The registrar's office maintains records of a student's performance at Mount Merry that are available to the student for a small fee at any time after graduation. Graduates requiring a transcript for potential employment possibilities may contact School Comptroller Izzy A. Shyster to have such transcripts sent (and, for a somewhat more substantial fee, altered).

FRESHMEN

Freshman registration takes place after upper-class registration, and owing to the demand for certain courses, freshmen should be prepared to sign up for their eighth-or ninth-choice courses, at best. Many freshmen choose to satisfy their distribution requirements at this time and take the two required courses, which are always available. Freshmen having difficulty finding open courses are directed to the History Department in general, and to Prof. Kingston Mildew's courses in particular.

A daylong period of orientation precedes registration for freshmen. The day's activities include: a double-time tour of the complete campus, perusal of the extensive orientation and registration information, attendance at opening lectures by Dr. Kaiser and Dr. Fitzcox and at Nurse Aurelia Slouch's "adult disease roundup," a Passion play mounted by the Holy Office, and a mandatory chapel service with reception to follow (Episcopalians need attend only the reception). Orientation festivities conclude with a "dance" at the Padded Cell. Students often form intimate bonds on this first night.

GRADING SYSTEM

Mount Merry uses a unique grading system devised to accommodate the caliber and abilities of its students. The grades assigned are as follows:

ASS	Academically Superior Studies
COW	Commendation on Work
PIG	Passing, if Garden-variety
PU	Passing, Unsatisfactory
F--K	Failure: Unforgivable Classroom Klutz

These grades are assigned according to the Quality Point scale. Quality Points will be given for perfect attendance at classes, neat handwriting, clean desks, papers bound in pretty plastic covers, and erasing the blackboard.

INCOMPLETES

Students are expected to fulfill all requirements to the satisfaction of the teacher. The grade of incomplete is assigned only when, as a result of unusual or entertaining circumstances (e.g., flash floods), a student is unable to complete any or all of his course work. In such cases, the student petitions for a grade of incomplete in lieu of a failing grade and the instructor subsequently devises a series of chores, academic or otherwise, which the student must perform in the ensuing semester. If the student is not in residence during that term, the instructor will consider the conditions met and will assign a grade arbitrarily.

THE PASS/FAIL OPTION®

Students may elect to take courses for a grade or under Mount Merry's own Pass/Fail Option®. The Pass/Fail Option® was created to inspire a sense of adventure in students and to encourage them to meet the challenges of courses that they might not get good grades in. With the freedom of the Pass/Fail Option®, students may plan their schedules with abandon, not worrying about the consequences.

It should be noted that grades of "P" may place students at a competitive disadvantage when applying for admission to graduate or professional schools (but then, so does attendance at Mount Merry).

REPEATING COURSES

If a student feels he has not fulfilled his maximum potential in a given course he may take it again, as often as he likes. While every attempt will be counted toward the nineteen units required for graduation, only the best final grade will be recorded on the student's transcript.

POSTING GRADES

Following an old Mount Merry tradition, grades are publicly posted by student's name, in order of class rank, in the student center. Students who are dissatisfied with their grades may take up the issue with the individual instructor during the Contention Period that follows the Grading Period.

ACADEMIC STANDING

In order to maintain good academic standing at Mount Merry, the following conditions must be met:

1. A student must maintain a cumulative grade point average with at least one digit to the left of the decimal point, unless the student elects to take all of his courses under the Pass/Fail Option®;
2. A student must be satisfied with his progress from semester to semester;
3. A student's choice of courses should bear some relationship to his chosen major;
4. A student must be enrolled;
5. Tuition and all other fees must be paid in full.

The records of all students are reviewed at the end of each semester. If a student has failed to comply with conditions #1–4, his records will be altered to his advantage. If, however, he has failed to comply with condition #5, his account will be turned over to a collection agency.

EXAMINATIONS

Examinations are given in all courses at the end of each term, unless the instructor concerned decides he can't be bothered and gives out grades according to any method that amuses him. Students schedule their examinations themselves within the period designated by the academic calendar and may take them in any setting that proves most beneficial to them.

ARCHAEOLGY

Grades are posted for students' convenience.

All tests and examinations are given under the Honor System, and all students must sign the Honor Pledge when handing in an exam. Any violation of the Honor System constitutes a serious offense, and any student who infringes on the Honor Code will be turned over to the Holy Office if he is caught.

LEAVE OF ABSENCE FEATURE (LOAF)

Mount Merry's Leave of Absence Feature (LOAF) is a planned interruption in a student's educational program. Under this system, a student voluntarily determines to drop out of college for an unspecified amount of time. The program allows students to reevaluate their educational goals, earn additional money, travel, and/or gain other practical experiences not available on campus (such as surfing, fishing, and hitchhiking).

The principal advantage of LOAF is that it offers the student the opportunity to leave college temporarily with the assurance that he will be able to return and resume his studies with a minimum of administrative difficulty. The student is able to be away from the college while maintaining close ties with the college community because he continues to pay full tuition and dorm fees (the college does reserve the right to sublet his dorm room).

PREMATURE WITHDRAWAL (Academia Interrupta)

Students who wish to pull out before the consummation of the term should notify the administration beforehand so that the college can distinguish them from the numerous students on LOAF. It should be noted that withdrawal entails a permanent break with Mount Merry and students who later change their minds and wish to re-enroll will have to submit to the rigorous admissions process all over again. Students who want portions of their tuition and other fees to be refunded upon withdrawal must meet one of two qualifications:

1. Withdrawal for compelling health reasons (must be certified by Nurse Aurelia Slouch);
2. Withdrawal for compelling economic reasons (must be approved by School Comptroller Izzy A. Shyster).

In either case, the final decision concerning the refund rests with the appropriate school representative.

GRADUATION HONORS

Graduation with honors at Mount Merry may be achieved by outstanding accumulation of Quality Points for superior work in the classroom (see Grading System). Four levels of honors are recognized at Mount Merry: summa cum laude, magna cum laude, cum laude, and approxima cum laude.

The Dean's List is compiled at the end of each term by the Office of the Deans to acknowledge students who have achieved distinguished academic records. To be selected for this honor, students must receive four letter grades in the course of the term, including "P" or "F."

The highest academic award at Mount Merry is the Mildred Maim Scholarship Award, founded in 1954 by Mrs. Maim in honor of herself. A panel of judges selects five semifinalists of each sex from among the contestants nominated by the faculty. The ten semifinalists are judged on superior academic achievement, talent, poise, beauty, and congeniality. In a colorful pageant held at the Waterbury Holiday Inn, contestants parade before the panel of judges in the famous Swimsuit and Evening Gown competitions. The final selection is made after each student answers a special meaningful question about a topic of world importance. Last year's question was, "What would be your advice to world leaders?" In a poignant finale, winners are decorated with the distinctive tiara, sash, and scroll of the Mildred Maim scholars, which they wear to their classes and all school functions in the ensuing year. Runners-up for each sex will assume the tiara, sash, and scroll in the event that the Maim Scholars elect to participate in LOAF or Premature Withdrawal.

PHI BETA KAPPA

Phi Beta Kappa is a national honorary scholastic society open to men and women with superior achievement records. Selection is based upon faculty recommendations, grade records, and the breadth of the student's overall program. There is no chapter at Mount Merry.

I PHELTA THI

I Phelta Thi is an honorary society organized for the purpose of upholding the principle of a liberal arts education: the broadening of the mind by direct contact with the many fields of human knowledge. The membership is chosen from a limited number of upper-class women on the basis of their character, personality, charm, and aesthetic sensitivity. As well as showing perfunctory interest in the intellectual growth of the college throughout the year, the society assists the Lecture Committee in encouraging attendance at lectures, plays, and concerts, and in arranging hospitality for, as well as personally servicing, visiting speakers.

PHOTO BUG

Greek Row.

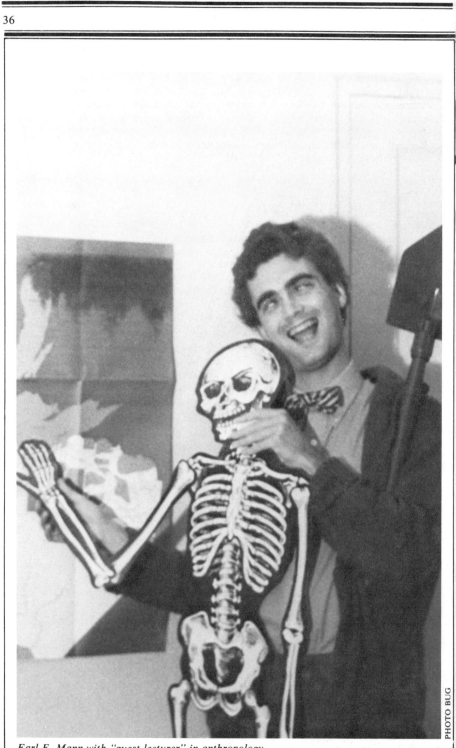

Earl E. Mann with "guest lecturer" in anthropology.

PHOTO BUG

DEPARTMENTS AND COURSE LISTINGS

ANTHROPOLOGY

Anthropology is concerned with the dynamics of human interaction throughout the world for the past four million years, as well as right here at Mount Merry. Anthropology is broken up into five subfields: Ethnology—an understanding of the diversity of human culture, including those who don't wear underwear; Social anthropology—the structure of human society and man's social climbing; Archaeology—a look at past cultures through their material remains which are analyzed and marketed; Linguistics—the history, formal properties, and tyranny of language and how it can be used for social stratification; and Physical anthropology—the biological diversity of man through time, evolution, adaptation, and weight loss. Some of these subfields are offered at Mount Merry for students interested in a broad grasp of the variations and kinks within the human condition.

Anthropology is an ideal major for persons who plan to work with people, especially those from unfamiliar backgrounds. Students develop an understanding and maybe even tolerance of diverse cultures, including their own. Research centers on comparing one society to others separated from it in time and space in order to find out who and what's regular and irregular. As the head of the department, Prof. Earl E. Mann, says, "Anthropology—it's just digging your fellow man!"

Requirements for the Major:

A major in anthropology must take Practical Archaeology (ANTHRO/B.C.–1) and then either take four more courses in the department or register artifacts worth $100 or more with School Comptroller Izzy A. Shyster.

ANTHRO/B.C.–1: PRACTICAL ARCHAEOLOGY

A survey of the methods, techniques, and data of contemporary salvage archaeology. Studies in archaeological research and business are available for students at the college's archaeological excavation site at the Waterbury Refuse Park. Past examples of excavated finds include arrowheads, Indian pottery, old issues of the *Saturday Evening Post*, and a 1956 Maytag dryer. Prerequisite: School Comptroller Izzy A. Shyster's permission and registration fee.

EARL E. MANN

ANTHRO/1066–2: SOCIOLINGUISTICS

Linguistic categories and their relation to culture—how to tell if someone's a snob, a hick, a bimbo, or just an idiot. Attention will be paid to regional and social dialects and sex-linked speech including double entendres and innuendos. Vocal mimicry and ventriloquism will be studied as social activity and effective party games.

LORD PENNYLACKING

ANTHRO/1066–1: PEASANT SOCIETIES

Students learn the internal political processes of preindustrial agrarian social systems by recreating the living conditions of those societies at the rear of the campus. Basket weaving, hut building, bread baking, water toting, and taking care of livestock will be featured. Course consists of professor's lectures; class discussion not permitted.

LORD PENNYLACKING

ANTHRO/B–52: CULTURAL SEXISM

A consideration of cultural expectations about male and female behavior in both traditional and modernizing societies. The roles of men and women in the family, community, and class structure are explored ethnographically in discussions devoid of sexual antagonism or bias. Enrollment limited to men.

COL. ULYSSES HAWK

ANTHRO/100G's–1: CHANGING AFRICA

From the British Empire to the Triangle Trade, the historical and contemporary efforts of Western countries to manipulate the Dark Continent's economic structure are examined. Particular emphasis will be placed on Alex Haley's *Roots* and the process of making money off ancestors.

LAMBERT GLIBB

ANTHRO/π:
ANTHROPOLOGY AND
MODERN LIFE

Students learn to apply anthropological techniques to the patterns of modern life. Some themes examined will be: tribalism, kinship, elitism, language, and political organization. Final project will be examination of a close-knit unit of Mount Merry life, such as the Ranology Department, with close attention paid to their uppity ways.

IRVING KLUPFERBERG

ANTHRO/#5:
STATUS AND POWER

Emphasis is on emblems of status and power in modern American culture, especially urban. What is the significance of a Mercedes 450SL? A Betamax? A corner office? A Rolex watch? Special topics in the past have included lunch techniques, the implications inherent in a street address, telephone manners, and reverse snobbism. At least one entire seminar will be devoted to the question of blue jeans. Special guest lecturer: Michael Korda.

FRANK LLOYD KOVALCHICK

ANTHRO/100G's-2:
ANTHROPOLOGY OF
TOURISM

A consideration of the society that produces the touristic impulse (i.e., nineteenth century America, twentieth century Japan) and the desirable qualities of favorite touring spots (i.e., good shopping, exciting night life, gorgeous natural vistas, and mind-improving culture). Does man travel to prove his superiority? To broaden his horizons? To meet chicks? To have the pleasure of coming home again? Attention will be paid to the political, social, and economic impact on host cultures, and the ethical implications of consistently cheating tourists.

LAMBERT GLIBB

ANTHRO/B.C.-2:
HUMAN EVOLUTION

Where did we come from? A spirited examination of one of man's oldest questions. With due respect to Biblical theories, students will debate the chicken and the egg question, Darwinian theories, and some of Dr. Leakey's more spectacular discoveries. Not recommended for practicing Catholics.

EARL E. MANN

ANTHRO/10k:
ETHNOBOTANY

The interdependence of people and plants, and cultural variations in that relationship. The course discusses the uses of plants in religious and intellectual life, from fig leaves to Rastafarianism. We will not limit ourselves to leafy plants, but will also discuss the implications of fungi and succulents as exposed in the writings of Carlos Castaneda, among others. Also examined: the social significance of the lawn (eradicating crabgrass), the vegetable garden (what to do with all that zucchini in August), and bringing people flowers.

MAJOR PUSHER

ART AND ART HISTORY

Art is a barometer of human experience and of the psychic economy of individuals and society, and no full understanding of it is possible without studying the functions and meaning of human art-making. At Mount Merry this is achieved through study of the history of art and exhaustive examination of artistic techniques. In the historic mode, a student places himself in past and faraway civilizations without a plane ticket; he comes close to the heart of a culture. He learns a great deal about its philosophy, technical accomplishments, ritual, home-life, eating habits; he sees and touches the artist's original object; and he pays for it if he breaks anything. Amid the constant social revolution of our time, the Art Department provides a program whereby students understand the timeless soundness of art as an expression and as an investment. While artistic theory is scanned, students reach a degree of intuitive facility whereby appreciation of a work of art is achieved quickly and irrevocably, without reference to academic art criticism.

In the art studio, students learn to see before they learn to draw—often by being blindfolded and then being instructed to fondle representative art works. A studio artist with sensual skills is well prepared to perceive sensitively his own times. The governing Art Board is committed to making the practice of studio arts available to as many non-art majors as possible who can meet the price.

Because art is one of Mount Merry's perennially popular departments, thanks to the instructors' supportive and lenient class structure, it is relatively free from the competition that often plagues art departments at other schools. Frank Lloyd Kovalchick, department chairman, is a practicing artist in search of local, national, and even international recognition. The facilities consist of an art studio space in the Art Center, whose museum features, in the Klumpp Memorial Wing, a tile-for-tile recreation of a 1950s kitchen and rec room. Also tucked into the Art Center are a woodworking studio which shares time with Cub Scout Troop #13 of Waterbury, and a clay/plaster studio furnished by School Comptroller Izzy A. Shyster's Surplus Task Force. For photography students, two darkrooms may be found in the Student Union, although many students find they get more reliable results from Spiro's Camera Nook, located in the shopping center just outside the school gates.

Although Mount Merry does not have an extensive permanent art collection, Prof. Irma Feeley possesses a library of more than 150,000 full-color slides, many of which depict art. These slides are used in class, and may also be borrowed for individual study or for parties by arrangement with Ms. Feeley. Students are encouraged to travel during their vacations to art galleries, both for the opportunity to observe art at firsthand and also for the chance to meet attractive people with similar interests. Since art majors acquire an appreciation of beauty, both in art and in the rest of the world, this department is recommended for those who wish to work in gallery management, picture framing, and home decorating.

Requirements for the Major:
Students will be accepted for major standing only through petition and submitting portfolios of selected work to the Art Board. All submitted work should be recent and reasonably original, although it should be noted that the faculty is disinclined to handle *wet* oil and finger painting, or freshly thrown pots. The faculty seeks students demonstrating intensity of involvement, potential for development, and affiliations with major artists and galleries. The department may retain student work for exhibition and sale.

ART/4 to 6–1:
INTRODUCTION TO ARTS AND CRAFTS
An introductory course in the basic principles in drawing and ceramics. Students learn how to draw, finger-paint, watercolor, make plaster-of-paris molds of their hands, make pot holders, weave baskets, make ash trays, iron leaves between two sheets of wax paper to make placemats, and perform other utterly valueless endeavors. Prerequisite: your own jar of Play-Doh.

MRS. ROGERS

ART/4 to 6–2:
COLOR IN ART
The prints and drawings of masters, including Dürer, Daumier, Matisse, and Dine. How do you like them as is? Would you like them better if they were in color? Would you like to find out? Students use Venus pencils and crayons to color Xerox copies of famous prints. Penalty points for coloring outside the lines. Art show at term's end provides commercial opportunities.

MRS. ROGERS

ART/CT5334–62–78:
VISUAL PATTERNS IN NATURE
A psychological and philosophical consideration of why forms in nature and art are often similar. Do you think the artist copied nature? Do you think he should be able to get away with it? Examples will include Van Gogh's *Starry Night*: Is he kidding? Whoever saw a sky like that? Was he on drugs?; El Greco's *Crucifixion*: What? This guy needs his eyes examined!; and Duchamp's *Nude Descending a Staircase*: No wonder she's nude! What kind of dress could fit a weirdo body like that? She shoulda stayed upstairs! No previous art background necessary.

LEON DE THUGG

ART/1066:
THE SOCIAL POSITION OF ARTISTS
A study of the changing public image of the artist. Students review the sorry lives of Amedeo Modigliani, Gustave Courbet, and Henri de Toulouse-Lautrec and contrast them to the more glittering examples set by Peter Paul Rubens, John Singer Sargent, and Andy Warhol, who made all that painting pay off—in a big way. Topics will include hot-button market strategies and predilections of gallery owners and museum curators.

LORD PENNYLACKING

ART/69:
THE MALE NUDE

An appreciation of one of nature's marvels—the naked man! From Michelangelo to Rodin to *Playgirl*, the male nude has fascinated artists and this course is a loving, firsthand examination of the subject, touching on torso, contrapposto, biceps, triceps, pectorals, deltoids, latissimi dorsi, gluteus maximus, and other highlights. Models will be selected from the student body. Prerequisite: examination by the instructor.

IRMA FEELEY

ART/#5-1:
PROBLEMS IN MODERN AMERICAN ARCHITECTURE AND URBAN PLANNING

What is the architect's responsibility to his client? the developer? the site? the contractor? posterity? This course attempts to answer some of these questions and attack such thorny issues as reflective glass facades, ostentatious historical reference, and white as the color of choice. Field study in downtown Waterbury addresses none of these problems, but is required nonetheless.

FRANK LLOYD KOVALCHICK

ART/#5-2:
CREATIVE PHOTOGRAPHY

An introduction to photography as craft and art form. Course is divided into a practical approach to the camera (cameras are placed on tables, students walk up to them and are introduced to lens, shutter, light meter) and an appreciation of great photographic work (from Francis Frith to Francesco Scavullo). Attention will also be paid to retouching, airbrushing, and photomontage for maximum impact.

FRANK LLOYD KOVALCHICK

ART/#5-3:
TRENDS AND MOVEMENTS IN APPLIED AESTHETICS

The cyclical nature of taste dictates that yesterday's fashion is today's discard. Styles in decorative arts and folk art that have returned to vogue recently include Art Deco, Art Nouveau, and Victorian; this course attempts to predict what will become fashionable next. Under consideration are most stylistic trends of the last 30 years, including themes such as hairy textures in upholstery, extensive use of the color orange, and plastic. Course examines artifacts from the Klumpp Memorial Wing of the Art Museum.

FRANK LLOYD KOVALCHICK

ART/#5-4:
MODERN AMERICAN ART

American art since World War II. What did the artist mean? Why did he use such ugly colors? Why can't we tell what he's painting? Who's good, who isn't, how to tell when a painting's upside down, comments *never* to make in a museum, what to say when in doubt, names of collectors, critics and artists (with pronunciations), and recent prices paid for their work.

FRANK LLOYD KOVALCHICK

ART/$3:
AMERICAN DECORATIVE ARTS

Fine and ordinary furniture, ceramics, rugs and lamps; decorating trends from Goddard-Townsend to Sister Parrish to neo-modernistic. Attention will be paid to the undecorated look, the "colonial Williamsburg" look, the "Mediterranean" look, as well as the extensive creative possibilities inherent in wall-to-wall shag carpeting, spiral staircases, exposed brick, and ferns. Classes will be held in the Klumpp Memorial Wing of the Art Museum.

REV. BRUCE CADEMYTE

BIOLOGY

Biology is simply "the study of life" and Mount Merry's Biology Department proposes to give in-depth coverage of the many different kinds of lives possible—insect, amphibian, plant, mammal, autobiographical. Each course should enrich the student's general background and provide him with an improved understanding of how his body works and what every part of it is for—through explicit demonstrations. In addition to learning about themselves, students will become acquainted with animals and plants and how they fit into our environment, especially in the home. Students may plan a curriculum appropriate to filling the minimal requirements for the B.A., or, under their professors, they may lay the groundwork for an advanced degree. Through the gracious generosity of the Ranology Department, facilities include occasional access to the $8 million Ranology Center. The school infirmary offers opportunities for internships comparable to on-the-job training.

Requirements for the Major:
Students must take Introductory Biology (BIO/409) and Elementary Frog Studies, and may elect to take Our Bodies, Our Selves (BIO/69) or arrange for personal counseling with Prof. Irma Feeley. At least twelve hours per semester are required in the workshop lab, as the faculty believes that students acquire awareness of biological principles through laboratory experiences and escapades. Students wishing to retain lab specimens for personal culinary use may barter with School Comptroller Izzy A. Shyster.

BIO/409:
INTRODUCTORY BIOLOGY
Introduction to the science of living things, plant and animal. Attention will be paid to the principles and method of biology, particularly dissection and vivisection. Prerequisite: high school biology taken in the last eight years, or mental examination by the professor.

PROCTER GAMBLE

BIO/π-2
STRUCTURAL BIOCHEMISTRY
The application of the principles of organic and physical chemistry to the study of biological systems. The course provides an understanding of biochemistry important to those students considering postgraduate study in medicine when they grow up. The laboratory work includes a study of the structure of macromolecules by spectroscopic, hydrodynamic, electrophoretic, and chromatographic methods as well as by conjecture.

IRVING KLUPFERBERG

BIO/16.2:
EQUINE SCIENCE
A study of the horse's functional anatomy, reproduction, common ailments, and the eternal appeal to prepubescent girls. Special emphasis will be placed on breeding, grooming, and stable management. The course will consist of three hours of lecture and discussion and a weekly laboratory, which includes field trips and mucking out after Flicka, Misty, and the instructor.

MR. ED

BIO/1,000 V:
GENETICS
A study of classical genetics and the principles of inheritance—bone structure, coordination, baldness, and blue eyes. Topics include mutation, recombination, DNA structure, and cracking the genetic code. Class discussion will touch on genetic engineering and its investment potential.

NORMAN BATES

BIO/π-1:
EROTIC NATURE
Reproductive habits of metozoans, coelenterates, platyhelminthes, aschelminthes. Special attention will be paid to foreplay among rotifers, nematodes, and hematomorpha. (This course formerly entitled "Invertebrate Behavior.")

IRVING KLUPFERBERG

BIO/4 to 6:
BASIC HUMAN ANATOMY
Students learn that the foot-bone's connected to the ankle-bone, the ankle-bone's connected to the shin-bone, the shin-bone's connected to the knee-bone, and so on. Oral examination at course's end.

MRS. ROGERS

BIO/1776:
THE ANIMAL KINGDOM
Constitutional monarchy as it functions among mammals; parliamentary procedure for dumb beasts, the problem of the figurehead monarch, and determining the ultimate identity of the king of the forest.

KINGSTON MILDEW

BIO/69+8″+et al.:
OUR BODIES,
OUR SELVES:
HUMAN REPRODUCTION
With workshops; permission from professor required, enrollment limited to mammals. Pharmacy fee.

IRMA FEELEY,
BRUNO COXMAN
AND STAFF MEMBERS

BIO/1967:
PLANT BIOLOGY
Frequently-asked questions about plant life: how often to water? is repotting necessary? when to feed? Special topics include the effects of music and reading aloud on plant growth, grow-lights, and plant medicine (what does it mean when the leaves fall off?). The approach is practical, rather than theoretical, in nature.

GRETCHEN INDIGO

BUSINESS

"THE BUSINESS OF AMERICA IS BUSINESS," a great American president once said, and this dictum becomes a creed at Mount Merry. The faculty of the Business Department is dedicated to giving students the instruction they need to make it in today's marketplace. Both trade and industry are explored for their commercial possibilities and the potential for private income they offer. Students also research the nature of private enterprise—procedure, policy, payola—and attention is paid to business interest, concern, and responsibility (should they be met or shirked?). Students are required to supplement their course work by participating in some kind of commerce on campus; students with entrepreneurial aspirations are taught how to mind their own businesses. These enterprises contribute to the Mount Merry community in many ways. Among the cherished college landmarks is the crowd of eager business students selling junk food to math majors, hawking packets of No-Doz at Kingston Mildew's history lectures, and maintaining the Cliff Notes Lending Library for Classics and English majors. Head of the department Hugo Markup proclaims, "Good business is making them an offer they can't refuse," and recommends the major to students who plan to have an occupation after graduation.

Requirements for the Major:
All majors must take the courses taught by Hugo Markup or arrange a private deal with him.

BUS/100%-1:
QUANTITATIVE METHODS
The use of quantitative analysis in business is introduced. Topics include index numbers, input-output analysis, elementary decision theory, as well as how to count the change at the end of the day, how many dimes are in a five-dollar roll, and marking "sale" prices that are the same as the regular price.

HUGO MARKUP

BUS/III:
BUYING BEHAVIOR AND MARKET DECISIONS
Analysis of markets and grocery stores as they influence consumer reactions. Why little old ladies never seem to be able to maneuver their shopping carts. What to do when the date on the milk cartons was yes-

terday's. The effect of Muzak on shopping. Why people with twelve items always get on the express line. How do those cashiers press the buttons with those long fingernails. How you wind up with the one box of tampons without the price so that the cashier must wave it in the air. Reading includes: *People* magazine, *Reader's Digest, TV Guide,* and *Family Circle.*

H.A.G. KLUMPP

BUS/7-11:
ELEMENTARY CASHIERING
Verna says: You can study and become a cashier in only two weeks. Then you can get a job, earn steady pay, have flexible hours, and meet people. Opportunities await you: supermarkets, drugstores, chain stores, bowling alleys, etc.

VISITING PROFESSOR WITH THE
RANK OF LECTURER
VERNA

BUS/90 lb.:
BUSINESS COMMUNICATION
A survey of basic means of communication. Students learn how to use a typewriter: how to put the paper in, how to change the margin and the tab, how to get the White-Out out of clothes. Elements of the business letter: the proper form and how to forge the boss's signature. Operating the switchboard and intercom system and the effective ploys of putting customers on hold or "accidentally" disconnecting them. No educational background necessary.

CASPAR Q. WIMPLEY

BUS/100G's-1:
PLANNING AND PROJECTION FOR THE FUTURE
A course for majors and non-majors interested in business careers. Starting with long-range goals (how much money do you want to be making when you're fifty? where do you want to grow old and die?) and working backward to the present, students are guided in outlining a career path. The second half of the course focuses on the immediate steps: getting a haircut, buying a suit, polishing your shoes, and borrowing a briefcase for the interview. Course may be repeated until student finds employment.

LAMBERT GLIBB

BUS/12 oz.:
RISK MANAGEMENT
Risk in personal and business affairs; the different methods for meeting risk. The

principles of risk-reward ratios will be thoroughly discussed, and applied to such situations as investing in speculative stocks, playing blackjack, and crossing streets against the light. Students are expected to have some knowledge of odds, and some experience with a pack of cards.

DOWNING BEERY

BUS/1040:
TAX-FREE GIFTS
The economic benefits of giving money away. This course examines the theories and procedures behind large tax-deductible gifts. Tax brackets and IRS calculations to reach deductible percentage are studied thoroughly. Attention is also focused on the beneficiaries of such gifts, how the money may be put to use, and how much money is needed for a significant contribution, with special emphasis on Mount Merry's needs. Suggested contribution: not less than $5,000.00.

SCHOOL COMPTROLLER, IZZY A. SHYSTER

BUS/100%-2:
ENTREPRENEURIAL STUDIES
Do you have trouble working for other people? Have lots of ideas? Want to get rich? Maybe you should start your own business. This course covers procedures for obtaining seed money, incorporation, partnership, management techniques, selling out, bankruptcy, and starting over again. All levels of commerce from lemonade stand on up will be examined.

HUGO MARKUP

BUS/100G's-2:
INTRODUCTION TO
ADVERTISING
A hands-on course covering the principles and practices of advertising. Questions of audience, message, and medium are examined, but the large part of the course will be devoted to graphic design, copywriting, and the mechanics of purchasing space in print. Final project: Mount Merry's new ad campaign in the back pages of the *New York Times* Sunday magazine section.

LAMBERT GLIBB

BUS/19th:
PERSONNEL MANAGEMENT
Contemporary theory and practices relating to the management of people in an office. Psychological and physical techniques are discussed, along with questions of recruiting, compensation, and discipline. How to pick out the troublemakers in an interview situation. When firing is the only answer. What are the most desirable production conditions in the workplace—do long coffee breaks, personal photographs on desks, and relaxed dress codes really make workers happy? One lecture and three hours of typing and filing in the admissions department per week.

NATASHA GOLDMAN

CHEMISTRY

Chemistry is a primary science that is an important factor in technological, historical, and social progress, not to mention business. The Department of Chemistry strives to share with students the spirit, method, and some of the facts of the science. Courses offer options to satisfy students in a wide range of levels of study and consciousness. The field of study exposes students to both theoretical and practical aspects as well as to substances that can alter a student's whole concept of his being and purpose. In order to keep abreast of current trends in the field and to maintain market parity, the curriculum is frequently reviewed by the department's own faculty. Many major items of research equipment have been obtained by School Comptroller Izzy A. Shyster and both students and faculty are welcome to utilize them for a small lab fee. There are plenty of opportunities for independent research and it is not unusual for students to see their own original work published in research journals under the faculty's names.

A degree in chemistry opens many professional doors. Many students enter private drug industries and others work in law enforcement crime laboratories—often graduates in these two areas find their paths crossing after graduation. A number of our successful graduates have even made it into medical school. As department head Rob Rush has said in a common moment of enthusiasm, "Chemistry is great, man."

Requirements for the Major:
The requirements have been kept to a minimum so that students may tailor their programs to the needs of the faculty members. Advanced students often assist faculty members in research projects (frequently receiving financial remuneration as well as valuable experiences).

PHOTO BUG

Professor Rush conducts chemistry experiments that are relevant to modern life.

Enthusiastic chemistry students sample their product.

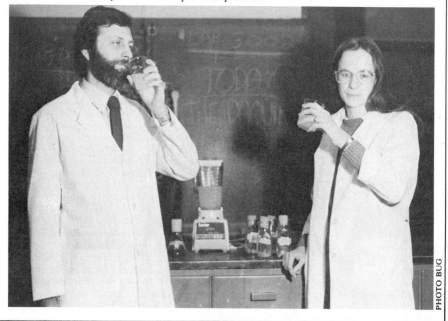

PHOTO BUG

CHEM/90 lb:
CHEMISTRY FOR THE LIBERAL ARTS

A survey of the basics of chemistry—formulas, elements, test tubes, and Bunsen burners. This course does not serve as prerequisite for any other course in chemistry, or any other department, for that matter.

CASPAR Q. WIMPLEY

CHEM/1:
ORGANIC CHEMISTRY

A practical study of chemical kinetics on the human biological system. Students will experiment with K-Y jelly, Vaseline petroleum jelly, cold cream, tanning butter, Crisco shortening, and any other substances on hand. Course loads may vary with individual students.

HARRY PALMER

CHEM/KP:
SENIOR CHEMISTRY LABORATORY

Students develop research projects based on the theory that a clean laboratory is a good laboratory. Three-hour practicum daily after all the other chemistry classes have finished using the lab. Cleanup techniques and practices supervised by faculty. This course may be repeated for credit *ad infinitum*. Prerequisite: a can of Comet cleanser.

CUSTODIAL STAFF

CHEM/10k:
CHEMISTRY IN LITERATURE

A course designed to introduce non-science majors to the important role of chemistry in great works of world literature. Lotions, potions, and alchemy are discussed, with stress laid on the possible composition of the liquid that made Juliet look dead, the contents of the little bottle that made Alice grow, and poisons in the work of Agatha Christie.

MAJOR PUSHER

CHEM/409:
CHEMISTRY IN ACTION

Applications of chemistry to daily life; field course with discussions. Trips to hospitals, factories, and nuclear laboratories planned; students must sign releases beforehand.

PROCTER GAMBLE

CHEM/250 mg:
RECREATIONAL CHEMISTRY

General theories of drug design and drug action. Discovery and development of natural and synthetic compounds having physiological and neuropharmacological effects. Includes attention to marketing and distribution methods.

ROB RUSH

CHEM/38D:
BIOCHEMISTRY AND WEIGHT LOSS

Biochemistry as it relates to metabolization of nutrients. Emphasizing the cell structure of proteins, lipids, enzyme action, and biological molecules. Weight loss of ten pounds or more guaranteed; fulfills the science requirement.

MARY DYCHE

CLASSICS

Classics is the study of the ancient civilizations of Greece and Rome, their culture, history, and language. But how does this relate to our modern world? The faculty attempts to demonstrate to today's students the relevance of ancient times by making our classical Western heritage accessible. Thus students can both share in its fabulousness and relive the good times of these great empires. Head of the department Rev. Bruce Cademyte favors a practical approach to the material, wherein students actually recreate the old customs and activities. Language studies, for example, teach students how to read and converse in the rich Greek and Latin languages (students at Mount Merry are often surprised by the connection between the Greek and Latin words and their English counterparts). However, literature courses listed under the rubric of "classics" do not presuppose a knowledge of either language: indeed, the faculty members themselves cannot recall ever seeing one of the texts in the original language.

Because students are unable to master all aspects of antiquity, they select the area of concentration that interests them most—patrician or plebeian—and are treated accordingly. Each course is divided into sections, and seating plans, assignments, and grades reflect each student's choice.

46

Requirements for the Major:
Each student designs his program and toga in conjunction with the head of the department. All majors must participate in the annual bacchanalia where grades are based upon students' performances. Although students may combine study of both Greek and Latin traditions, they should bear in mind that they may get very confused.

CLASS/B–52:
HOMERIC WAR CORRESPONDENCE
A concentration on the most overlooked talent of the Greek poet—his visceral, you-are-there approach to recording battles and combat. His influence will be traced to later works by Cornelius Ryan, Edward R. Murrow, Michael Herr, and the D.C. War Comics series.

COL. ULYSSES HAWK

CLASS/$3–1:
POLITICAL THEORY AND PRACTICE IN ANCIENT ROME
A review of the parliamentary procedure in the Roman Senate, the means of retiring a leader (specifically the case of Julius Caesar), the ways of attaining the title of emperor (see Claudius I), and the policies for maintaining peace and order as emperor (*vide* Caligula). Prerequisite: Students must satisfy the instructor's requirements.

REV. BRUCE CADEMYTE

CLASS/12 oz.–1:
ANCIENT COMIC TRADITIONS
A study of the ancient comic literature of Aristophanes, Plautus, Petronius, and Apuleius and how their gags have survived virtually intact in the later comedy of Mel Brooks, John Belushi, Dom DeLuise, and Federico Fellini. Class meets in dining room for weekly food fight.

DOWNING BEERY

CLASS/12 oz.–2:
CLASSICAL MYTHOLOGY
An investigation of the classical myths in their cultural context and in their particular application to parties and revelries. Students will reenact such popular rites as a Dionysian celebration, a Liberalia festival, a bacchanalia on Greek Row, and Maenads' Night in the women's gym (male students' attendance optional). Prerequisite:

no background necessary but students better be able to hold their liquor.

DOWNING BEERY

CLASS/B.C.:
GREEK AND LATIN ROOTS
An introduction to etymology, examining common Greek and Latin bases for words in English and other languages. Useful for people entering the medical professions and people wishing to be obnoxious at parties. Also studied: Greek and Latin names for radishes, carrots, turnips, parsnips, and rutabaga.

EARL E. MANN

CLASS/1066:
WEALTH AND POVERTY IN GREECE AND ROME
From ancient times to the present, a detailed examination of the financial patterns of Greece and Rome. What did the ancient Romans spend all their money on—those banquets? Were the poor people in Greece as clean as they look in all those pictures? How do the prices on the Via Veneto compare to Madison Avenue? Some attention will be paid to the phenomenon of the Greek coffee shop as pervasive financial model.

LORD PENNYLACKING

CLASS/$3–2:
CHURCH LATIN
In English. A study of the Latin used in pre-Vatican II church rituals, with special attention paid to ecclesiastical pronunciations. Students will learn to recite the Latin mass by heart, sonorously, and will also be exposed to key phrases, Latin tag lines, and book titles. The course will be taught by rote, with no consideration of grammatical structure or understanding.

REV. BRUCE CADEMYTE

CLASS/1776:
ATTIC GREEK
An investigation into the puzzle of the attic. Do you understand what's in yours, or is it Greek to you? The main thrust of the course is devoted to deciphering the origins and significance of all those unidentifiable objects in your attic. May also be applied to cellars or spare closets.

KINGSTON MILDEW

CLASS/1,000 V:
GREEK TRAGEDY

An introduction in the themes and characters of Greek tragedy. Students learn once and for all who was married to whom, who slept with whom, who made the gods mad and why. Special mnemonic techniques enable students to identify and keep straight the versions by Sophocles, Aeschylus, and Euripides. Class will put on one play, using ketchup as a substitute for blood.

NORMAN BATES

CLASS/69:
THE ROMANTIC LATIN TRADITION

The Latin Lover, myth and reality. How did Latins get such a reputation for being good lovers? Is this reputation based on fact, fiction, or their extensive use of brilliantine and their pencil mustaches? Valentino, Ricardo Cortez, Don Ameche, and Fernando Lamas are among the cases studied. Further course material will be drawn from the writings of Helen Lawrenson and the extensive personal experiences of the professor.

IRMA FEELEY

COMPUTER SCIENCE

Computer science is a discipline that deals with the major issues of representation, transmission, communication, electroprocessing, and other sesquipedalian terms that make the speaker sound smart. Especially recommended for students who don't like people, computer science opens up a whole new realm where the only feedback you get is what you yourself programmed. Areas of interest include the properties of surfaces and pictures (which sure beats reading) that appeal to students of both natural and artificial intelligence.

Introductory courses help nonmajors learn the role of computers in society and the problems of living with them if you don't know how they run, how to turn them on, and so on. An important aspect of computer science is learning the significance of extracting information for a purpose. Information processing is as much a part of nature as motion and energy and is a dandy way of guaranteeing that you'll pass every exam.

Mount Merry looks forward to the acquisition of a computer to augment the pocket calculator which is currently run on an open shop, self-serve basis. Private, cozy time-sharing terminals are widely distributed all over the campus and are always available to majors for study or to nonmajors for necking purposes. The computer lab has a workshop in which students may construct small computer systems, peripheral hardware, stereos, or zip guns.

Requirements for the Major:
All majors must wear black-rimmed glasses, carry slide rules and pocket calculators, wear plastic pocket protectors in their short-sleeved shirts, and tote around bulky black Samsonite briefcases with secret combination locks. No outside reading is required, but majors must have seen *Star Wars* at least eighteen times.

CS/69:
COMPUTERS IN PSYCHOLOGY

A survey course on the use of computers in forming personal relationships. Students submit personal data and are assigned dates with whomever the computer matches them up with. Must be taken on a satisfactory/unsatisfactory basis. Further exploration of the application of electronic devices that heighten interpersonal relations will certainly be included.

IRMA FEELEY

CS/π:
ELECTRONIC CIRCUITS LAB

An introduction to electronics covering theory and applications of electrical circuits and semiconductor devices. Basic concepts of control and computers and their maintenance, upkeep, and repair. Intensive three-hour lab in Fernquist Math Center. Students must provide their own tool kits and be prepared for emergency repair assignments at any moment of day or night.

IRVING KLUPFERBERG

CS/00:
ADVANCED COMPUTER SYSTEMS

Planning, strategy, and technique of computer games on an advanced level. Computer golf. Computer baseball. Computer auto racing. Special attention will be paid to the effect of environment on eventual outcome; evening laboratory takes place at the Padded Cell. Prerequisites: winning six straight games of Space Invaders with instructor.

STEVE E. DORE

CS/90 lb:
NUMERICAL ANALYSIS WITH A PROGRAMMABLE CALCULATOR

Introduces basic techniques for carrying out basic numerical analysis. Addition, subtraction, multiplication, and their practical applications will be discussed. Students are required to demonstrate some digital dexterity to guarantee they can press the right buttons on their calculators.

CASPAR Q. WIMPLEY

CS/4 to 6:
COMPUTERS AND YOU

Hi. I'm your school computer. What would you like to know about computers? I'm working on it. Just a moment, please. Sign up for this course and we can continue. You'll find out that we computers can be very helpful in your life. If you have any questions, press the button and we can start all over.

MRS. ROGERS

CS/1,000 V:
ARTIFICIAL INTELLIGENCE

What makes computers smart? Are they smarter than men? Smarter than women? Study of the programs and techniques that allow computers to behave intelligently. Some attention will be paid to chess strategy, as well as checkers, backgammon, and Mah-Jongg.

NORMAN BATES

DEVELOPMENT STUDIES

Development studies is a systematic examination of the processes, prospects, and odds against the development of human and material resources. Because the problems of development are urgent, gigantic, and enormously complex, they transcend conventional academic boundaries and demand a totally free-form discipline depending on the student's individual need. For this reason, the program has a strong appeal to Mount Merry students, and the faculty strives to take advantage of the students' needs and open up opportunities for encounters on the most personal human level.

Constantly searching for insight into behavior, the members of the department hope to influence students by exciting their intellects, ripening their capacities for sound judgments, redefining their values, and assisting them in their movement toward self-actualization and satisfaction. Often, students find that they understand themselves better, grow as a result of the courses, and gain a healthy respect for the diversity of human behavior and neuroses. Among the multifaceted issues met head-on are the possibility of emotional and intellectual growth; changes throughout the life cycle and what can be done to cover them up; social forces which can affect behavior and how they can be manipulated; and what—if anything—makes man unique in this world.

The O'Kays, co-chairmen of the department, help students set up a schedule of courses relevant to today's world. In the procedural aspects of organizing a plan of study, students in the program are invited into a "caring community" consisting of The O'Kays, participating faculty members, the students' faculty advisers, teaching associates and assistants in the program, and other curious recruits.

Requirements for the Major:

Majors must write a thesis listing in graphic detail all the major and minor conflicts and problems in their own personal and sexual development and how they have overcome their guilt and inhibitions and learned to seek new forms of awareness and contact. Efforts are not rated on the basis of numerical grades. Instead, students will receive handwritten evaluations of what beautiful people they are.

DS/250mg:
STRESS

Are your parents nagging you about your grades or your spending too much money? Does your roommate bounce a basketball in your room constantly? Do you find it difficult to remove the child-proof top from the aspirin bottle? A practicum for students needing a stress outlet. Vocal release is offered as a preliminary approach, with advanced studies in mixing Valium, Librium, sodium Pentothal, and Quaaludes as available.

ROB RUSH

DS/50/50–1:
DECISION MAKING

Every day we are confronted with questions in which decisions must be made. Should I get out of bed? Should I brush my teeth before eating breakfast or afterward? Should I borrow my roommate's clothes because I don't have any clean ones? These and other decisions are tough to make. What counts is fidelity to your real desires. The purpose of this course is to stress the need for the individual to express *his* or *her* needs—the importance of not losing sight of the self in making decisions. Through such self-centeredness, the most personally rewarding decisions can be made.

THE O'KAYS

DS/38D–1:
BODY IMAGE AND THE AESTHETIC EXPERIENCE

A review of the importance of body image and body experience for psychic life. An examination of the aesthetic experience in its relation to the body with emphasis on the empirical questions that have been and can be derived from existing data and theory. What influence do cellulite, acne, or just plain ugliness have on your enjoying life? Should you go to a fat farm, have dermabrasion, sign up for plastic surgery? These are questions you will have to answer, as every student is forced to stand before a full-length mirror in a leotard and be evaluated by classmates.

MARY DYCHE

DS/69+8″:
INTERPERSONAL SEXUALITY

An examination of how we relate to each other as sexual beings. A survey of the sexual habits of fellow members of the animal kingdom will throw light on sexual interaction devoid of such human characteristics as personality, temperament, and guilt. Students will come to a better understanding of basic human needs and will be able to communicate on new levels they had never previously dreamed possible. Satisfaction guaranteed.

IRMA FEELEY and BRUNO COXMAN

DS/90 lb:
COORDINATING SEMINAR

A seminar to synthesize knowledge acquired from other classes in the college. Students learn practical practices such as placing divider tabs in spiral-ring notebooks, using different colored index cards for different subjects, the invaluable nature of yellow highlighters, arranging school books on a shelf by the Dewey decimal system, and keeping a class schedule card. Especially useful for students who would like to be organized even when they're out of school.

CASPAR Q. WIMPLEY

DS/B–52:
LEISURE EVALUATION AND COUNSELING

What do most people do with their spare time? Could they be using it better? This course examines recreational habits and the desirable effects of leisure time: lowered blood pressure, a greener lawn, a first-rate collection of baseball cards, for example. Attention is also paid to convincing other people that they should be using their time better. Television will be discouraged on principle.

COL. ULYSSES HAWK

DS/50/50–2:
PERSONAL GROWTH

Offered as independent study.

THE O'KAYS

DS/38D–2:
HUMAN POTENTIAL

An honest attempt to make students live up to their potential in intellectual, moral, and physical terms. Through a variety of approaches such as TM, est, Rolfing, group therapy, Silva mind control, re-birthing, Esalen, and Scientology, students are coaxed, bullied, hypnotized, and browbeaten into improvement. Numerical grades based on quantitative progress.

MARY DYCHE

DS/14th:
FEMALE DEVELOPMENT

Making the transition from the traditional male imperialist power structure to a liberated egalitarian cooperative; the administration of Mount Merry College is taken as the laboratory. Techniques will include strident argumentation, humorlessness, withholding sexual favors, and not shaving. Course closed to men.

NATASHA GOLDMAN

DS/50/50–3:
VALUES CLARIFICATION

An in-depth examination—and possibly restructuring—of students' value systems. What is most important: money, your family, or a cure for cancer? When you think about your future, do you imagine that you'll have access to a sizable income? Would you give any of it to charity? Course teaching method consists of multiscreen presentations from which students choose the most important item, e.g., an ice cream cone, a Porsche, or a blood bank.

THE O'KAYS

EASTERN STUDIES

The Department of Eastern Studies concerns itself with the civilizations of the Far, Middle, and Near East. Specialized courses throw light on art, religion, and culture—including the funny clothes they wear (especially the men's dresses)—in an attempt to make the inscrutable East a little more scrutable. Since there is only one introductory course in the languages of these countries (all of them) offered at Mount Merry, the department's comprehensive body of information is accessible to all. In keeping with the more severe aspects of Eastern philosophy, Chairman Doo Wop has designed a rigorous and inflexible interdisciplinary program to provide students with a keen idea of life in Eastern culture, while giving them at least a minimal familiarity with each country, making them glad they grew up in America.

The strength of the program lies in its special focus on the balance of Western and Eastern trade, like the fact that lots of fancy French boutiques have stores in Jidda. Many of the instructors have prepared their own textbooks and teaching materials from their personal observation, research, and conjecture about the East; they can usually offer students highly reasonable rates on these materials. Finally, Chairman Doo Wop has been instrumental in establishing various Eastern dinner nights in the dining halls which give students a taste of different culinary approaches to leftovers, while saving them the inconvenience of leaving the campus or calling for take-out.

Requirements for the Major:

All majors must participate in the department's annual production of *The King and I* (with Chairman Doo Wop as the King and Gretchen Indigo as Anna), for which they will be required to dye their hair black and wear it in pigtails.

In their final seminar projects, students must immerse themselves in the culture of a chosen Eastern country (for OPEC nations, limousines may be rented from School Comptroller Izzy A. Shyster), and, wearing costumes, participate in the annual Chinese New Year parade in downtown Waterbury, which culminates in a banquet at McDonald's followed by the traditional costume-burning bonfire in the Municipal Parking Lot.

ES/100%
THE EASTERN MARKET

An economic survey of the modern Eastern market with tips and consumer information on transistors, stereo components, compact cars, Persian rugs, caftans, and contraband. Prerequisite: valid passport, all shots, interview with School Comptroller Izzy A. Shyster.

HUGO MARKUP

ES/280Z–1:
BYZANTINE HISTORY
You figure it out.

DOO WOP

ES/#5
CONFLICT AS NUANCE IN THE EASTERN FILM

A comprehensive look at the popular film genres of Eastern culture, particularly the "domestic dramas" of Bruce Lee and Sonny Chiba. The films will be studied principally as social documents and thought will center upon why the masses cram themselves into theatres to watch these obviously fake exhibitions of martial arts and gratuitous gore. Emphasis will be placed on the Japanese methods of resolving conflict and the Indian tendency to make movies that go on for hours. Required reading includes subtitles.

FRANK LLOYD KOVALCHICK

ES/III:
PROBLEMS IN EASTERN GASTRONOMY

A practical approach to Eastern dining. How to use chopsticks. What exactly is the difference between chop suey and chow mein? How to tell if the food contains MSG. Should you eat curry if you don't like hot food? Is the falafel sold on the street safe to eat? Is it ever polite to eat with your fingers? Do they really eat raw fish? Field trips to Eastern dining establishments in the Waterbury area or take-out.

H.A.G. KLUMPP

ES/69:
LOVE IN EASTERN CULTURE
Close examination of selected works and customs representing the various Eastern approaches to *l'amour*: Kama Sutra, Japanese erotic art, Turkish baths, and Oriental massage. Enrollment limited to capacity of football stadium.

IRMA FEELEY

ES/280Z–2:
BASIC EASTERN STUDIES
Students become acquainted with the locations of the Near East, the Far East, the Middle East, the Eastern Bloc, and the East River, and develop at least a minimal familiarity with some of them.

DOO WOP

ES/$3:
INTRODUCTION TO CHINA
A survey course designed to acquaint students with the fundamentals of china. Principles of place settings and open stock, bridal registry, patterns both formal and informal, as well as advisability of dishwashing. The properties of stoneware, bone china, porcelain, and melamine are compared. Special topics covered may include: Royal Crown Derby, Spode, Herend, Limoges, and Ginori, with one session on compatible crystal and silver patterns. Recommended reading: the pertinent sections of Amy Vanderbilt's *Guide to Etiquette*.

REV. BRUCE CADEMYTE

ES/747:
ELEMENTARY EASTERN LANGUAGES
Students learn the alphabets and basic sentence structure of many Eastern languages, often including Arabic, Hebrew, Persian, Chinese, Japanese, and Hindi. Owing to the variety of the languages, the course requires final exams every two weeks.

PEPE LE PUE

ES/B–52:
WOMEN'S ROLE IN THE EAST
Roles of the woman in Eastern culture: the odalisque, the houri, the geisha, the mental-

ity of the harem. Are eunuchs necessary? Attention will be paid to the woman's place in the modern Eastern home. Enrollment limited to men.

COL. ULYSSES HAWK

ECONOMICS

Many of the social problems facing the world are rooted in the economy. The Economics Department is designed to: introduce students to economic theory, acquaint them with some economic institutions, instill basic skills in applying economic analysis (to contemporary issues as well as to depreciation on a motorcycle or the tax benefits of a burned-out warehouse), and create a foundation for intelligent citizenship *or* shrewd business acumen. Broadly defined, economics is the study of the governing of the allocation of scarce productive and mental resources among a variety of uses. More specifically, students achieve economic literacy useful for understanding current affairs and sales tax tables in addition to satisfying their curiosity about how society can solve the problems of organized productive effort—if it really wants to.

Under the experienced guidance of Department Chairman Lambert Glibb, students get an insider's view of the complex economic forces at work in the behavior of the firm, the consumer, and the policies of government, and how they can be manipulated. By grasping the disciplines of accounting and microeconomy, students may learn the benefits of creative bookkeeping.

No specific high school preparation is required as all courses are taught at the introductory level. In fact, Chairman Glibb prefers "students who are green. That way, they're open to more progressive ideas about handling money." Economics majors tend to take one of two paths upon graduation. Some enter directly into the economic market while others go on to graduate school indefinitely. The department is renowned for preparing students for professional and graduate examinations, thanks to Chairman Glibb's pamphlet, "101 Ways to Pass Any Test."

Requirements for Graduation:
Students who do not possess a knowledge of certain mathematical and statistical techniques may be required to pay a higher registration fee. All students enrolled must take at least one course in computer science

to gain awareness of how costly those contraptions are for the office when they always break down. Majors must work a minimum of eight hours a week at the comptroller's office in accounting and cashiering each semester to receive the degree. Advanced degrees are negotiable with the department chairman.

ECON/B–52:
SOVIET-TYPE ECONOMICS

How the Russians save their money in a Communist society, considering that their salaries aren't that high to start with. Queuing up, the black market, making sure the country has enough money for those missiles. What do blue jeans cost in Moscow? What is the rent on the average *dacha* in the country? How can those poor Russians afford all that vodka?

COL. ULYSSES HAWK

ECON/100%:
GEMSTONES AS INVESTMENT

A practical course in the financial aspects of gemology, including grading of stones, cutting, setting, and flaws. Attention will also be paid to taxes, insurance, appreciation. Special focus on engagement rings. Scholarship students not accepted.
(ALSO HE/100%)

HUGO MARKUP

ECON/40:
ECONOMICS AND RELIGION

What the Catholics do with all that money. Special emphasis on investments in real estate and the morality of being a slumlord; the spiritual appreciation potential of fine art; and the uses of precious gems and metal in ecclesiastical *objets de vertu* such as chalices, thurifers, and pectoral crucifixes. Materials fee: A collection plate will be passed in class.

REV. MOSES SAVONAROLA

ECONOMIC JUSTICE

Not offered this year.

ECON/III:
MODERN ECONOMIC THOUGHT

A survey course that examines the currents of the economy as interpreted by Galbraith, Malkiel, Samuelson, and Heloise: from supply and demand to coupon clipping. Special emphasis will be paid to the effect of interest rates on meatloaf.

H.A.G. KLUMPP

ECON/100G's–1:
DOLLARS AND CENTS

Introduction to the very basis of American economy. What is that pyramid on a dollar bill? Whose portrait does a $50 bill feature? What three words appear on every coin? Includes examination of pocket change up to a $100 bill. Materials not included.

LAMBERT GLIBB

ECON/100G's–2:
PERSONAL FINANCE

A systematic review of the many tax loopholes available to citizens. Emphasis on how to write off your food budget, house, recreational vehicles, and insurance policies as business expenses. Attention will be paid to balancing checkbooks, keeping keys separate from change, carrying a plastic coin purse, and managing debts in a creative fashion. Prerequisite: Dollars and Cents (ECON/100G's–1).

LAMBERT GLIBB

ECON/CT5334–62–78:
SOCIO-ECONOMIC POLICY

Analysis of the role that money plays in a social and financial arrangement—like a date. Should the guy bring something to her, like flowers or chocolate? What if he forgets his wallet; should she bail him out? Should the girl offer to go Dutch? Who's responsible for the costs of transportation? Of birth control?

LEON DE THUGG

ECON/00:
ECONOMICS AND SPORTS

The effect of sports on the individual's economy. Which stadium seats give you the most for your money? How much can you get for an autographed baseball? How those scalpers rip you off. And all those brands of running shoes—how to pick the right pair for you at a price that you can afford.

STEVE E. DORE

EDUCATION

The Education Department is designed for students who want to be teachers. For the best possible understanding of the learning process, students must experience an environment that mimics their future students' experience. To this end, Mount Merry's program offers the revolutionary approach of using elementary school teaching methods on its education majors, in their junior year.

Students interested in or needing early childhood education will follow this elementary program and will be rewarded daily for good work and obedience during naptime with gold stars by their names. Diplomas are awarded upon accumulation of sufficient gold stars. The endlessly patient department chairman, Mrs. Rogers, has achieved remarkable results in her handling of millions of children and Mount Merry juniors. "Can you do that?" she often says to her students. Frequently, they can.

By senior year, students are expected to grow up and assume an adult role in the educational transaction. They are exposed to and practice teaching approaches such as split-second assessment of a student's learning potential and diplomatic transfer of slower children to another class. Stress is also placed on the capacity for continual reappraisal of the teacher's personal objectives in education, the determination required to achieve them, and the reinforcements for this dedication that take the form of alcohol, amphetamines, and controlled daydreaming.

Requirements for the Major:
Students must evince competence in reading and writing. The program maintains a participative relationship with the Waterbury school system where student teaching is a five-day weekly assignment. Majors must take Self-Defense (PE/CT5334–62–78–2) before undertaking student teaching and are required to write a research paper on their experiences in Waterbury. Past research has included the study of adolescent alienation, drop-out rates, make-out spots, most reliable dealers, and favorite T.V. shows. Cross-matriculation in another college's undergraduate education program is suggested, as Mount Merry's does not fulfill the Connecticut certification requirements—or those of any states—necessary for a provisional teaching certificate.

ED/CT5334–62–78–2:
DELINQUENCY AND GANGS IN SCHOOL AND SOCIETY
A review of empirical studies of student violence and vandalism as related by guest instructors—The Sharks. Theories of youth delinquency will be demonstrated and practiced. It is recommended that all students taking this course leave valuables on campus. The class is held under Watertown Avenue Bridge. Students must pass final initiation test.

LEON DE THUGG

ED/19th:
EDUCATIONAL PSYCHOLOGY
A consideration of effective psychological principles applicable to learning: humiliation, ridicule, sarcasm, scorn, contempt, violence. Emphasis on such areas as human growth, development, motivation, and their manipulation. Compulsory two-day group experiences demonstrating basic techniques of the rack, iron maiden, Chinese water torture. Limited to prospective teachers and bullies.

NATASHA GOLDMAN

ED/90 lb–1:
TEACHING HEALTH IN ELEMENTARY SCHOOL
Insight into aspects of teaching health to children who haven't reached puberty. Basics such as brushing teeth, combing hair, and flushing afterwards will be stressed. Students who report cavities will be sent home to Mommy.

CASPAR Q. WIMPLEY

ED/4 to 6–1:
INDIVIDUAL DIFFERENCES IN CHILDREN
This course will examine the major kinds of differences in children: girl from boy, blonde from brunette, tall from short, smart from slow. A special advanced session is available for those students who have to teach identical twins. Much illustrative case material is utilized.

MRS. ROGERS

ED/CT5334–62–78–1:
STUDENT TEACHING IN WATERBURY
Students gain experience by operating in real classrooms with real live subjects. Study includes observation, supervised practice teaching, driving directions to the schools and nearby bars. Prerequisite: Self-Defense (PE/CT5334–62–78–2).

LEON DE THUGG

ED/4 to 6–2:
COMMUNICATING WITH PRESCHOOLERS

Hi. What's your name? That's a nice name. This course is all about communication. Can you say that? Com-mu-ni-ca-tion. That's right. That was very good. Would you like to sign up for this course? Can you write your own name all by yourself? Good, then you're big enough to take the course. I know you'll like it. We'll have fun. Do you like to jump rope?

MRS. ROGERS

ED/1:
TEACHING CHILDREN'S LITERATURE

Comic books, *TV Guide*, *Mad* magazine, pilfered *Playboys*, the novels of Carolyn Keene, Judy Blume, and Terry Southern. *Not* included: *Highlights* magazine, A.A. Milne, Maurice Sendak, *The Happy Hollisters*, and *The Bobbsey Twins*.

HARRY PALMER

ED/90 lb–2:
METHODS AND MATERIALS

Calling roll, maintaining discipline, coping with the short attention span. Techniques suggested include reading out loud, skits, classroom pets like guinea pigs, and corporal punishment. We will examine such materials as chalk, blackboards, construction paper, white paste, and crayons. Applicable to the teaching of *any* subject on *any* level.

CASPAR Q. WIMPLEY

ED/38D:
GRADING

The theories and applications of grading practices: letter grades (including plus or minus), number grades (on a 0–100 scale), and comments (in one, three, or five sentences). Averaging test grades, homework grades, and classroom performance. Dealing with the fat kid, the nerd, the cut-up, and sexual attraction between (or to) the little ones. Some stress will be laid on appropriate response to irate parents.

MARY DYCHE

ED/4 to 6–3:
ADULT EDUCATION

How to teach grown-ups—maintaining the interest level of people your parents' age. What to do if they don't do their homework; making the course work relevant (Run, Sammy, run!), adequate punishment/reward systems for students in a 50% tax bracket.

MRS. ROGERS

ENGLISH

The purpose of the English Department is threefold: to introduce basic written and oral communication in English, to instill an awareness of the existence of English and American literature, and to direct the major to personal enrichment and a chance of a career after college. First, since the ability to speak and write is a vital part of communication, students seek to acquire a command of language, particularly standard American English. Once a student has mastered the rules of grammar, it is possible for him to transcend textbook examples and enjoy genuinely free, human self-expression by forming sentences all by himself and understanding their meanings.

Secondly, majors learn that literary works are human art. Students become acquainted with Shakespeare, Milton, and other talented writers in order to appreciate their cultural backgrounds, question the connection between art and life, comprehend the human condition as reflected by people who think, and finally to broaden their sheltered lives through vicarious experiences.

Thirdly, the major should discover the liberating qualities of the imagination. On term papers, he can draw upon the inspiration of celebrated writers, either from literature or from the work of former Mount Merry students (found in extensive files on fraternity row). Students develop a discriminating appreciation of literary masterpieces and their subsequent condensations. By nurturing an affinity for books and reading, students prepare themselves for such careers as library scientist, receptionist, and lifeguard.

Study abroad is a common and enriching adjunct to academic education, and many Mount Merry students eagerly take advantage of the Liverpool Semester Program. Desirous of direct contact with the English language, they are never disappointed. Upon stepping off the boat in the famous port city, they are exposed to eye-popping variations on the language. They often return to Mount Merry with an enlarged appreciation of foreign cultures as well as such tangibles as "mod" Beatle wigs and colorful Liverpool accents.

PHOTO BUG

A Mount Merry student discovers literature.

Requirements for the Major

Majors must demonstrate an acceptable level of ability in English composition before graduation. Permission to postpone the completion of the competency examination may be granted, upon petition, by Department Chairman Caspar Q. Wimpley, who is very flexible with students who are firmly resolved to obtain their degrees.

Students may fulfill course requirements by achieving a score of five on the College Board Advanced Placement Examination in English, or by successfully completing the crossword puzzle in the Sunday *New York Times*. Each major must take three seminar classes in junior and senior years. Seminar classes consist of three hours of discussion with the instructor and students are warned to bring lots of coffee. It should be stressed that work outside of courses, self-initiated and self-sustained, is a vital ingredient of this major and that, by doing homework, the student constructs a foundation of knowledge which will withstand the shock of the unknown or the not immediately familiar on the final exams.

ENG/100%–1:
MODERN DRAMA

The giants of the modern theater—Miller, Chayefsky, Simon, Slade. Attention must be paid to box office successes, long runs, theater groups, themes that appeal to middle-aged businessmen who make up the bulk of the Broadway audience, and the inevitable choices for the Pulitzer Prizes for Drama. Required reading: the reviews of Clive Barnes.

HUGO MARKUP

ENG/1967:
MODERN POETRY

GRETCHEN INDIGO

ENG/100's–1:
CREATIVE WRITING

An introductory course designed to help students of every level of proficiency become competent writers, especially in terms of composition, organization, and strategies of invention. Students will develop skills in writing resumés, job applications, love letters, and tax forms. Plausibility will be stressed.

LAMBERT GLIBB

ENG/$3:
THE LYRIC VOICE

From the sixteenth century to the present, including Wordsworth, Coleridge, Shelley, Keats, Hart, Harburg. Attention will be paid to lyric interpretation, especially by song stylists like Judy Garland, Liza Minnelli, Barbra Streisand, and others. All examples heard from the professor's private collection.

REV. BRUCE CADEMYTE

ENG/1967–2:
MARITAL COUNSELING THROUGH POETRY

A seminar which focuses on the marital problems of Elizabeth Barrett and Robert Browning, and their ways of working these problems out in an honest, nonrecriminatory, caring fashion.

GRETCHEN INDIGO

ENG/1776–1:
THEOLOGICAL ENGLISH

How to write prayers; for students intending to enter the priesthood. Will be offered if anyone signs up.

KINGSTON MILDEW

ENG/100G's–2:
THE MODERN AMERICAN NOVEL

Best-sellers since 1975—Irwin Shaw, James Clavell, Judith Krantz, Harold Robbins. Lectures will emphasize critical and financial implications of turning books into mini-series, the importance of the mass market paperback, and naming real life characters while narrowly avoiding libel suits.

LAMBERT GLIBB

ENG/B-52:
GREAT BOOKS OF THE WESTERN TRADITION

A survey of the major works and themes of western culture. Texts include the novels of Owen Wister, Louis L'Amour, Zane Grey, Edna Ferber, and others.

COL. ULYSSES HAWK

ENG/100G's-3:
VERY FAMOUS AMERICAN WRITERS

Hemingway, Fitzgerald, Capote, Mailer, Vonnegut: the importance of the party circuit in the writer's career path. How to get invited, selecting a dashing wardrobe, making sure you're photographed, being prepared with witty quips, spelling your name for the gossip columnists, choosing the appropriate mate(s). The authors' work will be considered in context.

LAMBERT GLIBB

ENG/1776-2:
EARLY POETIC MASTERS

A course that covers readings in the early masters of English poetry: *Beowulf, Sir Gawain and the Green Knight,* and the complete works of Chaucer, Shakespeare, Milton, and Spenser. Students gain at least a passing knowledge of the output of the authors. Breadth, rather than depth of study, will be emphasized. Prerequisite: any speed-reading course.

KINGSTON MILDEW

ENG/4 to 6:
ELEMENTARY COMPOSITION

f u cn red ths sntnce y cn tak ths cors.

MRS. ROGERS

ENG/90 lb-1:
ENGLISH TRAINING CAMP

For honors candidates, a special session starting three weeks before the Fall semester. Workouts in the library using dictionaries, thesauruses, concordances, specialized encyclopedias, and critical matter. The value of primary source material such as letters and diaries is discussed, though Mount Merry's library doesn't own any.

CASPAR Q. WIMPLEY

ENG/90 lb-2:
XEROGRAPHY

A practical course in copying techniques, primarily Xeroxing. How to get the best, clearest copies, how to make your papers look longer, how to get the best deals, where to get enough dimes. Field study takes place in Waterbury's Xerox Copy Center.

CASPAR Q. WIMPLEY

ENG/90 lb-3:
PROOFREADING

How to make suree you're papers and examms are corre^{k}ly typped and Spelled. Looking things up in the dictnnary and taking out tpos so you Can get bedder Grades.

CASPER WIMPLY

ENG/1776-3, 4, & 5:
VERBIAGE

Long boring books: *Moby Dick, Sister Carrie* (unexpurgated edition), *Crime and Punishment, Remembrance of Things Past, Clarissa, The Magic Mountain.* Lab fee for No-Doz; course takes two years.

KINGSTON MILDEW

ENG/100%-2:
THE EPIC

Tracing the epic tradition from Greece to Hollywood. Homer, Virgil, Malory, and Cecil B. De Mille. Emphasis will be placed on running times, road show engagements, casts of thousands, inflated admission prices, and placement of the intermission. Prerequisite: The Gospel According to Hollywood (REL/100%).

HUGO MARKUP

ENG/1066:
BRUSH UP YOUR SHAKESPEARE

Shakespeare to quote in daily conversation. Special efforts are made to match appropriate quotations to common and unusual social situations. The goal of the course is to make you sound like a scholar. Primary text: *Oxford Dictionary of Quotations.*

LORD PENNYLACKING

FOLKLORE

Folklore springs from the most primitive level of man's fears and beliefs, and it is at that level that it is studied here at Mount Merry. Chairman Gretchen Indigo calls this department the most vital of all offered at the college because the subject "hits us all where we live—in the heart." Folklore deals with the sum of the culture of mankind as manifested in customs and creeds; for this reason it maintains vague ties to more creditable majors like anthropology, art, history, linguistics, music, philosophy, psychology, sociology, and any other discipline that prepares you for a real job. Cognate study in any of the above disciplines is highly desirable but not required because, after all, even uneducated savages can grasp the meanings in myth and voodoo.

Requirements for the Major:

Since folklore is a study of the humanist expression handed down by oral tradition rather than by writing, no reading whatsoever is connected with the courses. In order that majors may meet basic literacy standards, they must demonstrate proficiency either in reading or in putting hexes on their instructors. Students choose one of three areas for concentration: (1) Folk dancing, which requires demonstrated mastery of the watusi, the boog-a-loo, the Virginia Reel, and the funky monkey; (2) Folk art, which requires a thesis on either the meanings and motifs of bathroom graffiti at Mount Merry, or on the artistic significance of Fauntleroy's toy collection; or (3) Folk music, which requires that students analyze the basic human themes and concerns embodied in the music of Donna Summer, Barry White, Evelyn "Champagne" King, Millie Jackson, James Brown, and other latter-day muses.

FOLK/8″: SYMBOLISM

The ordering of experience through symbols in sundry cultural manifestations, such as art, literature, architecture, movies. Attention will be paid to Georgia O'Keeffe's orchids, the entire oeuvre of D. H. Lawrence, the Empire State Building, and the films of Douglas Sirk.

BRUNO COXMAN

FOLK/14TH: MAGIC AND WITCHCRAFT

A practical study of sorcery and the occult: taboos, divination, shamans, cargo cults, messianic movements, voodoo, and secret societies. Texts include: *Macbeth*, the Arthurian legends, records of the Salem trials, and Sybil Leek. Some ability in wax molding is presupposed. Prerequisite: séance with instructor.

NATASHA GOLDMAN

FOLK/¿: GYPSY STUDIES

The art of reading tea leaves, cards, palms, bumps, warts and wills, kidnapping children, writing ransom notes, smoking cigars, selling cigarettes, wearing gold earrings, and, in a pinch, selling off your sisters.

SISTER CONSUELA
CONCEPCIÓN IMMACULATA
DÓNDE ESTA EL LAVATORIO

FOLK/1967–1: IMPLICATIONS OF FOLK MUSIC

A cultural examination of the mysterious power over Caucasian liberals of dreary folk songs about racehorses, railroads, and weather conditions. Particular emphasis will be placed on the sartorial results of this music—Indian print skirts, granny glasses, sandals, headbands, leotards, and embroidered denim jackets. Review of the works of Dylan, Baez, Collins, and Ives. Limited to students who evince a strong degree of deep-seated guilt.

GRETCHEN INDIGO

FOLK/33⅓: MOTIFS IN AFRO-AMERICAN MUSIC

An investigation of the mythic imagery of Afro-American music, including such totems as reefer men, freak-outs, psychedelic shacks, the good foot, the Breaks, and Tutti-Frutti. Many questions raised by the material will be considered: When is Jimmy Mack coming back? What did she hear through the grapevine? Why don't Flo know if the boy she loves is a Romeo?

LEROI PAXTON

FOLK/10k:
THE WORKS OF CARLOS CASTANEDA

The Yaqui way of knowledge as imparted by a follower. Students will read Castaneda's entire oeuvre in the context of his life. Highlights will include tapes from conversations with Castaneda, slide shows of his desert home, and experiential contact with organic stimuli. Field trips in the professor's van will attempt to recreate the educational symbiosis of the master/disciple relationship with Castaneda.

MAJOR PUSHER

FOLK/1776:
PROBLEMS IN FOLK TALES AND LEGENDS

Why were the gods so tough on Hercules? Why was Arthur so dumb about Lancelot and Guinevere? How did Paul Bunyan feed Babe the Blue Ox, and how did Babe get to be blue? Did Johnny Appleseed really wander around with that stupid saucepan on his head? Weren't Sleeping Beauty's clothes out of style when she woke up?

KINGSTON MILDEW

FOLK/1967-2:
AMERICAN FOLK DANCING

Theory and practice of folk dancing from the American culture, viz.: why it's fun to stand in a circle and clap; how not to feel like an idiot; what to do when you get stuck with the ugliest person in the room. Folk dancing pre- and post-John Travolta. Dances examined include "Turkey in the Straw," "Virginia Reel," and "Hustle." Sneakers required; satisfies physical education requirement.

GRETCHEN INDIGO

FOLK/50/50:
RITUAL IN EVERYDAY LIFE

The ways we impose order on our fragmented lives with rituals. Attention will be focused on wishing (on stars, ladybugs, white horses, eyelashes, and pieces of pie) and averting bad luck (by throwing salt over the left shoulder and not walking under ladders), as well as setting the alarm clock, shaving, and feeding the dog.

THE O'KAYS

FOREIGN LANGUAGES

In this age when countries, in order to survive, must seek to understand each other, a command of a foreign language is a great advantage. Although most Mount Merry graduates do not become diplomats, many travel through Europe after graduation and they often remark that knowing a foreign language made the going easier, especially in the nations where the particular language was spoken. Thus, whether for trips abroad or for careers in the home, the study of a secondary language is invaluable for acquiring an appreciation of foreign people and their civilization through a study of their language, literature, arts, and wines and cheeses.

Mount Merry considers itself lucky to have a real foreigner chairing the department—Monsieur Pepe Le Pue of France who brings a continental flavor to the program with his beret, cravat, and cigarette holder. Le Pue has been instrumental in bringing many vestiges of European culture to the campus, including the widely-attended foreign language film screenings that have featured the films of Brigitte Bardot and Laura Antonelli. The gracious Le Pue has also made himself available for priate tutoring sessions for co-eds, often stretching into the "oui" hours of the night.

In reaction to student response, classes are small and many are taught in English. The department offers literature courses in translation for the students' enrichment and convenience. Students with advanced skills are hired as teaching assistants for lower-level courses, and sometimes they move up to full-time positions if Le Pue wants to take a week or two off. The department's comprehensive program offers a depth and breadth of courses which may include German, French, Spanish, Yiddish, and British. Extensive use of the language lab for practice is required for each course, though students should check the time schedule carefully beforehand in order not to interrupt confession. A wealth of recorded material is available for checkout in the lab, or students may prefer to play or cut their own records there.

Requirements for the Major:

Students must pass a final examination, or demonstrate the ability to pay a translator, to receive the B.A. (it is recommended, however, that students in the latter group at least learn to say "Please," "How much?" and "Where is the bathroom?" in their respective languages). Each Mount Merry student must take one course in foreign languages or endure Prof. Frank Lloyd Kovalchick's slide show of Europe. Living in the Foreign House does not satisfy the requirement, although for some students it may substitute for study abroad.

FL/You:
LANGUAGE LAB
Students are instructed in the operation and maintenance of the language lab situated in the confessionals of the chapels. Our seven-channel lab system offers French, German, Spanish, Italian, Latin, A.M. and F.M. stereo. Students may also record their own confessions and have them (or others') played back.

SELF-TAUGHT

FL/1066:
ADVANCED CONVERSATION
Preparation for students who wish to speak with elegance and erudition at faculty teas, interviews for fellowships, and meetings with students from other colleges. Areas of study include name dropping, literary allusions, interrupting, correcting, pronunciation, showing off knowledge of esoteric facts, and laughing too hard at jokes.

LORD PENNYLACKING

FL/π:
YIDDISH FOR GENTILES
If you don't know if you're a goy or shiksa, chances are you should be taking this course already. A study of the rich phraseology and exclamatory vocabulary for those who don't know schav from a shmuck. Final exam will take place over a Seder. L'chayim!

IRVING KLUPFERBERG

FL/747-1:
LA CUISINE DE FRANCE
(see HE/747-1)

FL/69:
ELEMENTARY CONVERSATIONAL FRENCH
Parlez-vous français? Oui, madame, un peu. Voulez-vous coucher avec moi?

IRMA FEELEY

FL/747-2:
THE LANGUAGE OF ROMANCE
How to court: sweet nothings, declarations, proposals, and propositions. Some attention will be paid to setting, delivery, the impression desired, and method, including Frenching.

PEPE LE PUE

FL/¿-1:
ELEMENTARY SPANISH
Conversational Spanish addressing the needs of the American tourist. Such terms as "dinero," "siesta," "No lo puedo," and the whole enchilada will be discussed along with other pertinent questions, e.g., Does a bull know what "olé" means?

SISTER CONSUELA CONCEPCIÓN IMMACULATA DÓNDE ESTA EL LAVATORIO

FL/747-3:
ENGLISH AS A FOREIGN LANGUAGE
Students learn to speak English as if it were not their native tongue. Emphasis will be placed on intonation, sentence structure, and accent. Final exam will be oral, entailing performance as well as translating the speech of such figures as Pia Zadora, Henry Kissinger, and Desi Arnaz. (This course highly recommended for residents of the Foreign House.)

PEPE LE PUE

FL/8″:
BODY LANGUAGE
How can you tell how a person feels about you—before he speaks? Students learn to interpret nonverbal messages such as anger, fear, aggression, hostility, and lust. What does it mean when a girl in a bar keeps her arms crossed? What about when she sits with her knees open? How can you express your innermost desires without saying a word?

BRUNO COXMAN

FL/#5:
STYLISTICS
A course to polish the foreign languages major in further cultural considerations so that he will be able to fit in abroad. Topics discussed include: men's jewelry, sports cars, hair coloring and style for both men and women, walking in four-inch heels (for both men and women), and double-breasted blazers. Models include: Mariangela Mela-

to, Marcello Mastroianni, Louis Jourdan, Catherine Deneuve.

FRANK LLOYD KOVALCHICK

FL/¿-2:
SPANISH CULTURE
An introduction to Spanish culture, its behavioral and grooming habits. Practice sessions in stamping feet, spitting, wearing exceptionally tight clothing and pestering American blondes. Women students may audit only, but not for credit.

SISTER CONSUELA CONCEPCIÓN IMMACULATA
DÓNDE ESTA EL LAVATORIO

GEOLOGY

Geology is the study of the earth and its development potential, a concept that students gain a canny awareness of through their work in this department. No one knows this better than department head (and Mount Merry alumnus) Storm E. Wether who claims he owes everything he is—and has—to mentor and School Comptroller Izzy A. Shyster. As an undergraduate under Shyster's tutelage, Professor Wether honed his lightning-quick and devastatingly accurate ability to assess the earth's richness, history, and future in quarter, half, and one-and-a-half acre plots. Students learn the wisdom of Professor Wether's favorite adage, "We can all profit from geology."

The geology faculty actively pursue their own professional interests and specialties in this field, such as starter homes, industrial parks, and speculation. Students may develop "apprentice" relationships with faculty members in which they aid in the instructor's research as much as possible without a license. Each major participates in the evaluation of his own work by grading himself as he sees fit. As a result, majors in this field have consistently had the highest GPA and average income in the college.

The varied faculty provide alternate ways of studying the earth, as each member views this subject in the broadest context possible. Basically, the department seeks students who are personable, confident, attractive, and looking for a major with a future.

Requirements for the Major:
All students must take Professor Wether's Geology Survey (GEO/72°F-1); quotas will be set after the first semester. Each major is assigned material for a senior project with which he must negotiate the best deal possible. Class standing is determined by final sale price.

GE/72°F-1:
GEOLOGY SURVEY
A practical introduction to Prof. Wether's principles of geology and their application in the field and on empty lots. Students are instructed in the techniques of surveying, looking up deeds, showing a piece of property to its full advantage, and closing. Course load includes off-campus work in Waterbury and the surrounding countryside. Students must provide own transportation.

STORM E. WETHER

GE/10k:
HISTORICAL GEOLOGY
An interpretation of earth history through the examination of the records of events recorded in rock from the pre-Pennsylvanian to the present day. Attention will be focused on the effects of Berry, Presley, Lennon, Jagger, Townsend, Hendrix, Springsteen, and others. Students will be asked to consider the perceptual difference of evaluating rock while stoned. Headphones required.

MAJOR PUSHER

GE/B.C.:
INTRODUCTION TO GEOGRAPHY
Students are taught where things are. Topics that might be included: the different hemispheres, the names of the five oceans, and the location of American Express offices. Chicago is in which state? Eskimos live where? What's doing in Ecuador? Where did they film *The Sound of Music*? Other questions will be answered.

EARL E. MANN

GE/12 oz.:
BEACH AND ISLAND
GEOLOGICAL PROCESSES
Processes affecting life on beaches and barrier islands with emphasis on keeping the sand out of bathing suits and beds, best hours for tanning, jockeying for position on the ferry, and effective pesticides and sunscreens.

DOWNING BEERY

GE/72°F-2:
WEATHER
Rain, snow, sleet, sun, wind, hail, clouds. Umbrella required.

STORM E. WETHER

GE/III:
SEDIMENTOLOGY
Physical processes and sediments of rivers, beaches, and deltas, as well as smaller bodies like ponds, bathtubs, and aquariums. Some attention will be paid to beverages like Turkish coffee and Alka-Seltzer.

H.A.G. KLUMPP

GE/$3:
PRINCIPLES OF PALEONTOLOGY
Examinations of the study of ancient organisms through fossil remains. Bette Davis, Gloria Swanson, Ann Miller, Ginger Rogers, and Nancy Reagan are among topics covered. Accent will be placed on man's intellectual recognition of fossils as organic remains via retrospectives, testimonials, life achievement awards, and roasts. The nature and possible causes of extinction will be considered.

REV. BRUCE CADEMYTE

GE/100%:
PETROLEUM AND ITS IMPLICATIONS
A study of the modern occurrences of petroleum, the methods used to locate, prove, and extract it (e.g., finer points of siphoning from 1973 Chryslers). Subjects covered in the past have included: what to do in long gas lines, how to entertain yourself when stationed in Jidda, Bahrain, and Abu Dhabi, and why Arab princesses have such bad taste in clothes.

HUGO MARKUP

HISTORY

History affords the opportunity to acquire a perspective on man's role in the universe and on earth throughout time. Department chairman Dr. Kingston Mildew brings a unique personal perspective to this field owing to his great age. In a characteristically candid accolade, Prof. Daisy McGillicuddy commented, "Of course he's a history teacher, he's lived it all since before the Civil War!"

The History Department at Mount Merry is the smallest department in the school. This intimate quality stems from Dr. Mildew's old-fashioned teaching and lecturing methods based heavily on students' memorization of historical dates and genealogical tables. His well-prepared, fact-filled presentations exclude class discussion and preclude class attendance. Drawing upon the example of an old mentor, "Early to bed, early to rise . . . ," Mildew habitually schedules the earliest classes in the school—lectures begin promptly at 7:45 A.M.

One of the oldest traditions of the department—indeed, of the school itself—is the course required of all Mount Merry students, History of Mount Merry College. Taught by college chaplain Dr. Kaiser, it is always heavily attended. The department's other offerings reflect the widely varied subject matter and enthusiasm of the instructors. Many of these courses involve reenactment of historical events or field trips on buses. At Mount Merry, most departments take their characteristics from the chairman, but the History Department is anything but dry and dull.

Requirements for the Major:
All majors must present evidence that they have attended Dr. Mildew's lectures at least once in their years at Mount Merry. An oral examination is required so that students may demonstrate their familiarity with such important historical data as: 1492, "Let them eat cake," the Confederate Army vs. the Union Army, which President the "teddy" bear was named after, Adolf Hitler, the Watergate Hotel, and the chronological order of Jackie Kennedy Onassis's husbands.

HIS/747:
FRANCE IN TURMOIL, 1789 TO TODAY
An overview of revolutions, Bonapartism, the Third Republic, the Fourth Republic, the Occupation, De Gaulle, the Fifth Republic, Pompidou, Giscard d'Estaing, Mitterand, the devaluation of the franc, the decline from supremacy of French fashion, the wine scandals of the sixties and seventies, major architectural mistakes in Paris, the lowering of quality and raising of cost of French bread, the increasing mediocrity of the films of François Truffaut.

PEPE LE PUE

63

PHOTO BUG

Colonel Hawk's gripping recreations of his favorite battles are the highlights of the History Department.

HIS/12 oz.:
ROMAN CIVILIZATION

A fond review of social structure, class, slavery, status and behavior of women, social organizations, and amusements in the Roman Empire, 70 B.C.–250 A.D., including banquets, baths, and orgies. Why they ate lying down, why they vomited between courses, and how they had chariot drag racing. Annual course highlight—reenactment of Colosseum program followed by toga party on fraternity row.

DOWNING BEERY

HIS/1066:
EUROPEAN SOCIETY

The social development of Europe from the casino at Baden-Baden to the beach at Biarritz. Special attention will be paid to American emigrés such as Henry James, Edith Wharton, F. Scott Fitzgerald, Nancy Astor, Consuelo Vanderbilt. A tour of the major houses of Europe, from Rothschild to Chanel. Specific focus on Prince Charles and Princess Caroline.

LORD PENNYLACKING

HIS/1967:
AMERICAN INTELLECTUAL
HISTORY SINCE 1975

A survey of modern exponents of intellectualism. Readings from Norman Mailer, Susan Brownmiller, Rod McKuen, Shana Alexander, Paul Harvey, Phyllis Schlafly, Joyce Maynard, Jesse Helms, and many others.

GRETCHEN INDIGO

HIS/69:
THE CONCUBINE AS
POLICYMAKER

The uses of pillow talk from Herodias to Eva Braun to Fanne Fox, with special attention to French monarchic tradition in the sixteenth and seventeenth centuries.

IRMA FEELEY

HIS/$3:
WOMEN AND ANTIQUITY

An examination of the causes and dynamics of the affinity between women and antiques. Special topics examined will be: the effect on French furniture prices of Marie Antoinette's lavish redecorating policies; the design of chairs as affected by female fashion; living with antiques in today's centrally heated homes; persuading yourself and your husband that those Queen Anne chairs are a good investment.

REV. BRUCE CADEMYTE

HIS/B–52:
WARS

An appreciation of some of the most glorious passages of world history through detailed examination of armed conflict. Among the topics examined are battle formations, strategy, uniforms, armor, guns and swords, planes and tanks, and beloved war leaders such as Attila the Hun, Napoleon, and General Patton.

COL. ULYSSES HAWK

HIS/00:
HISTORY OF LEISURE IN
AMERICA

Recreation as a means of self-expression in American society, starting with the Industrial Revolution and a cursory reading of Thorstein Veblen's *Theory of the Leisure Class*. The course's main emphasis rests on the leisure-time culture of the twentieth century and its artifacts. What does indoor-outdoor carpet say about us as Americans? What is the greater significance of successive fitness fads: bicycling, tennis, jogging and roller skating? What can we learn about our society from bean bag chairs? Do Frisbees mean anything? Course does not include reading.

STEVE E. DORE

HIS/π:
TRANSPORT HISTORY

An historical analysis of the movement of passengers and goods—the kinds of travel as evidenced in the artifacts of seaports, roads, train tracks, airports, and bus terminals. Interpretation of road maps, schedules, and travel agents' records will be heavily relied on to draw conclusions about travel patterns past and present, especially during national holidays.

IRVING KLUPFERBERG

HIS/1894:
THE HISTORY OF MOUNT MERRY COLLEGE

A topical and documentary investigation of Mount Merry from a small Catholic institution into a major center of liberal learning. The shapings of the college's purpose, function, and identity will be studied through the chaplain's Mount Merriana collections and personal recollection on the part of the aged staff. Classes subject to suspension without notice in case of absent-mindedness or college emergency.

DR. REGINALD KAISER

HIS/1776:
THE FUTURE OF NEW ENGLAND'S MILL TOWNS

Fall River, Danbury, Seymour; how they got that way and whether or not they can be saved. Is all this talk about "country chic" really true? Focus on real estate values and ethnic patterns of Connecticut River Valley. Field trip to Naugatuck.

KINGSTON MILDEW

HOME ECONOMICS

Although it has been argued that in this modern era of women's liberation, the science of home economics becomes less important, department chairman H.A.G. Klumpp disagrees. "After all, someone has to make a lovely home for every family!" she exclaims. She is very happy to see men of any persuasion enrolled as majors in her department. To her, this is evidence that there will be a larger proportion of lovely homes in the future. The occasion, three years ago, of the marriage of two home economics students, was almost too much for Miss Klumpp. "What a lovely, *lovely* home they'll have," she was heard to cry just before fainting into the wedding cake created by the departmental juniors.

The importance of home economics in the world and at Mount Merry is demonstrated by the wide variety of courses offered in domestic technology, the practical projects undertaken, and the reliance of the administration on the Home Economics Department to perform any number of important tasks on campus. Moreover, many of the home economics courses are offered in conjunction with other departments, proof of how integral they are to life on the whole and academic life specifically.

The home economics facilities at Mount Merry are the pride and joy of Miss Klumpp. Most of the cooking is done in the museum-quality, 1950's vintage Klumpp Sisters Memorial Kitchen, and the adjoining rec room is often the setting for lectures. The Klumpp Wing of the Art Center (where Miss Klumpp also makes her home) possesses such rare artifacts as a 1953 Hoover vacuum cleaner in perfect working order and an entire set of "Wheat Sheaf" motif melamine.

Requirements for the Major:

All seniors are required to take the practicum in addition to their normal course load. The practicum, four hours a week, consists of hands-on experience in home economics on the Mount Merry campus (see course description for details). All culinary-related courses carry the stipulation that students must consume their creations themselves. Students planning to have access to incomes over $50,000 yearly must take Domestic Management (HE/1066); otherwise, Market Policy (HE/III-2). Laundry Problems (HE/III-4) is recommended for the future wives of white-collar workers.

HE/1066:
DOMESTIC MANAGEMENT

Students address the servant problem. How to find good help these days. Fundamentals include the identification and functions of gardeners, chauffeurs, maids, babysitters, housekeepers, and butlers. Maintaining labor relations pertaining to wages, days off, and uniforms. Prerequisite: projected income over $50,000 or demonstration of career interests.

LORD PENNYLACKING

HE/69 + $3:
MEAT APPRECIATION

Students are instructed in the sizing up of choice meat: lamb, pork, veal, and beefcake. Emphasis will be placed upon the identification of the various cuts of meat with special attention to the versatile rump and breast sections, and to the desirability of firm flesh. A survey of hot dogs and meatballs may be included.

IRMA FEELEY and REV. BRUCE CADEMYTE

HE/KP:
INTERIOR ENGINEERING
A study of the operational mechanics of basic domestic products: vacuum cleaners, dishwashers, brooms, mops, dustpans, paper towels, sponges, and plumber's helpers. Individual labs at faculty residences. Course credit contingent upon passing the white glove test. May be repeated for credit, and eventually for minimum wage.

CUSTODIAL STAFF

HE/III–1:
HOME ECONOMICS PRACTICUM
Senior home economics majors put their skills to practical application on the college campus. Special projects in the past have included: setting up and maintaining a kosher kitchen, maintenance of the athletic department's uniform laundry, and sewing the gowns for graduation.

H.A.G. KLUMPP

HE/III–2:
MARKET POLICY
Choosing and patronizing the best supermarket on the basis of location, layout, quality of produce, name brands, and specials. Pinching fruit and shopping-cart technique will be covered, but the bulk of the course is devoted to finding, clipping, filing, and redeeming coupons.

H.A.G. KLUMPP

HE/747–1:
LA CUISINE DE FRANCE
A gastronomical tour of France, from *le potage* to *les noix*. Students are exposed to the ingredients, traditions, and techniques that made French gastronomy famous. Texts include Brillat-Savarin, Escoffier, and Julia Child. Highlight of the course: tastings of French fries, French bread, French toast, French dressing, French crullers, and French's mustard.
(Also FL/747–1)

PEPE LE PUE

HE/III–5:
MICROWAVE STUDIES
(see PHY/III)

HE/III–6:
GASTRONOMICAL GEOMETRY
(see MA/III)

HE/100%:
GEMSTONES AS INVESTMENT
(see ECON/100%)

HE/19th:
DOMESTIC CONTRACTS
(See LS/19th)

HE/III–3:
FOOD CHEMISTRY
The interactions of nutrients under various cooking situations. Texts include Betty Crocker, Fannie Farmer, and *The Joy of Cooking*. Specific topics include the effects of heat, cold, and whipping on flour, butter, eggs, and cream. Recipe writing and recipe following are stressed, with little heed paid to results.

H.A.G. KLUMPP

HE/III–4:
LAUNDRY PROBLEMS
From fine washables to ring around the collar, this course covers all facets of clothing maintenance. Issues taken up include: separate hampers for darks and lights, fabric softeners, ironing sleeves, the cost-benefit ratio of the commercial laundry, the psychology of the missing sock. Extensive practice in reading laundry labels on garments required.

H.A.G. KLUMPP

LEGAL STUDIES

In this era of litigation-prone citizenship, it's more important than ever to know how to obey the law. However, it is made increasingly difficult to do so as petty obfuscations cloud the meanings and imports of the law.

The Legal Studies Department is not intended to be a pre-professional course of study leading to law school (although at least three Mount Merry students in recent years have gone to law schools, one of which was accredited). Rather, it is intended to equip Mount Merry students to live at all times within the bounds of the law, if they choose to do so.

Most members of the faculty have had extensive in-court experience upon which they base little-known but foolproof tactics and strategies that students may find useful in their careers. Owing to the broad variety of topics covered, students planning any kind of career at all may profit from the courses offered in the department, and many students from other majors take Legal Studies courses as electives to learn the powers and, more importantly, the limitations of the law. "They're smart; they're covering their _____," says Daisy McGillicuddy, the able department chairman.

Requirements for the Major:
Based on the theory that experience is the best teacher, students will not be awarded a diploma until they have accumulated a court "record" in one of three fields of study—blue-, white-, or pink-collar crime. Potential majors should be alerted to the fact that they are responsible for their own court costs.

LS/9th pct.:
POLICE, LAW, AND SOCIETY
An appreciation of the social and historical origins of the police, their important role in the community, and the potential loss of their rights to frisk, to stop suspicious-looking characters, to enter and search, etc., by the action of civil liberties groups that are probably just mouthpieces for Commies. Lab fee: make checks payable to the Policemen's Auxiliary Local.

SGT. PAT O'BRIEN

LS/CT5334-62-78:
LAW AND THE RESOURCEFUL CRIMINAL
The seminar will explore the means by which a crafty felon may prepare his defense. Topics include insanity, incompetence, and the effects of a steady diet of Twinkies. A survey of financial possibilities after parole—book, movie and TV sales, religious and lecture circuit—and sound investments. Attention will be paid to the work of F. Lee Bailey, Percy Foreman, and "Racehorse" Haynes.

LEON DE THUGG

LS/100G's:
LAW AND THE SOCIAL SANCTION
What happens when society condones illegality: white collar crime, graft, tax evasion, extortion, mail fraud, and failing to use correct zip code. Case histories include Charles Colson, Steve Rubell, and Robert Evans.

LAMBERT GLIBB

LS/14th-1:
THE LAW THROUGH LITERATURE
Gaining an appreciation of how the law works from major milestones in the genre of court procedurals. Special emphasis on murder trials, with some attention to the operations of the police. Erle Stanley Gardner's work is stressed—the course reading will keep you on the edge of your seat! Note: This course does not cover corporate, commercial, or traffic law.

DAISY MCGILLICUDDY

LS/40:
LEGAL AND MORAL RESPONSIBILITY
Discussion centers on man's fall from grace and the necessity for laws, with emphasis on the Ten Commandments as guiding precedents. Cause, blame, guilt, punishment, fault, liability, excuses, justification, and scapegoats are covered. Not recommended for moral weaklings.

REV. MOSES SAVONAROLA

LS/19th:
DOMESTIC CONTRACTS
Premarital negotiations: alimony, palimony, galimony. Important points covered are who keeps the furniture, who takes out the garbage, who gets the kids. Some attention will be paid to the relatively new field of children's litigation. Although the work of Marvin Mitchelson will form the nucleus of the course, we will go back to eighteenth century marriage agreements for inspiration.
(Also HE/19th)

NATASHA GOLDMAN

LS/14th-2:
CITIZENS AND THE LAW
The function of law in society is to maintain order, hence the existence of minor laws governing individual behavior. This course examines the citizen's duty to obey these laws and the circumstances under which disobedience may be condoned. Situations under discussion include annoying blue laws, archaic sexual behavior ordinances, and the definition of a public disturbance, as well as the advisability of driving safely and obeying postal regulations.

DAISY MCGILLICUDDY

LS/100%:
INVESTING IN THE LAW
How to put the law to work for you; using your misfortunes and those of your family to make a buck. Malpractice, libel, and industrial liability, and the importance of asking high damages. Case studies include *Carol Burnett* v. *National Enquirer* and *People* v. *Ford Motor Company.*

HUGO MARKUP

MASS COMMUNICATIONS

Every day we're affected by the media in ways that we might not even have suspected. Why, even this catalog could be considered "medium." And media is what mass communications is all about—different ways to reach lots of people with a message, whatever that message is.

The Mass Communications Department is one of the most popular departments at Mount Merry, and one of the most easygoing. With his usual sharp observation, Department Chairman Downing Beery has often stated, "Mass communications are going on all the time." This means that students really don't have to go anywhere special or do anything particular to earn their degrees in this department. In fact, many majors complete their course of study without leaving their dorms.

The focus of most of the courses rests, not on the message, nor even on the workings of any particular medium, but, more basically, on its very existence and its nature. The essential simplicity of Professor Beery's character (and the profound simplicity of most Mount Merry students) guarantees that troublesome or complex intellectual issues will never be considered in the Mass Communications Department.

Requirements for the Major:
In order to graduate, students must attempt to demonstrate familiarity with some of the major tools of mass communications. They may do so by taking a well-balanced course load from the mass communications offerings, or by exhibiting proficiency in a manner of their own devising. Recently students have been awarded honors in the department for their work in identifying all the women in the Blackglama mink ads; singing along with an AM radio for an hour without missing any words of either songs or advertising jingles; and orally synopsizing the last twenty-six episodes of "General Hospital."

MC/90lb.:
INTRODUCTION TO MASS MEDIA
Students are introduced to such forms of the communications media as newspapers, magazines, radio, television, bubble gum cards, and skywriting.

CASPAR Q. WIMPLEY

MC/14th-2:
EFFECTS OF MASS MEDIA
The study of communication's effects on the constant television viewer. Do you think Walter Cronkite would make a good president? Do you think Barbara Walters asks hard-hitting questions? Do you have a crush on Tom Brokaw? Would you be afraid to let Mike Wallace into your home? Class lectures appear on Channel E at 3:00 P.M. Course work expected of students: the crossword puzzle in *TV Guide.*

DAISY MCGILLICUDDY

MC/8″:
VIDEO
A practicum in which students learn the basics of videotape: how to tell when the camera's on; which end of the camera you look through; how do you focus? Students tape their own programs which are broadcast on campus during early morning hours and at Waterbury's Notel Motel every twenty-four hours. Guest lecturers: Al Goldstein, Ugly George.

BRUNO COXMAN

MC/14th-1:
THE FIRST AMENDMENT—THE JOURNALIST'S BEST FRIEND
A practical survey of the law protecting journalists from libel and slander suits. Students learn how to override claims of invasion of privacy, defamation of character, copyright infringement, and violation of the Fairness Doctrine. Required texts: the *National Enquirer* and the *Star.*

DAISY MCGILLICUDDY

MC/12 oz.:
RADIO ANNOUNCING
An investigation of the role of the disc jockey. Special emphasis will be placed on the necessity for wacky nicknames, low humor, insulting the listeners during call-in contests, talking during the songs, and rushing through public service announcements so that they are incomprehensible. Attention will be paid to the financial considerations

of the job, including payola for plugging certain records and concerts.

DOWNING BEERY

MC/19th:
WOMEN IN MEDIA

Profiles of women who have made their mark in the mass media. Discussions include: Is Jane Pauley's hair natural? Where do Lucy and Ethel get all those costumes for the crazy stunts they pull? What was Mary Tyler Moore doing in Minneapolis? Can you believe Dinah Shore went out with Burt Reynolds? Are Suzanne Somers and Loni Anderson the same person?

NATASHA GOLDMAN

MC/1066:
HIGHBROW MEDIA

The principles of keeping media consumption well within the bounds of good taste, including an inquiry into the following questions: Why is the news that's fit to print so boring? How can I express my political convictions by the arrangement of reading matter on my coffee table? When is it all right to go to the movies (and is popcorn socially defensible)? What TV programs do intelligent people confess to watching? Does a Ph.D. in Comparative Literature excuse a confessed fondness for the novels of Jacqueline Susann?

LORD PENNYLACKING

MC/00:
MEDIA COVERAGE
OF SPORTS

Competitive sporting events hold a cherished place in the American psyche; the job of interpreting these events for the public is a taxing and controversial one. Among the subjects covered may be: why there's no regular TV coverage of croquet, how commentators think of things to say when there's nothing going on, who gets to go to the Super Bowl, and who supplies sportscasters with those rugs and ugly blazers.

STEVE E. DORE

MC/100G's:
HOW TO GET PUBLISHED

For those "in the know," the publications industry may seem like a happy family, but breaking in to get your stories published can be a daunting experience. This course deals with its practical aspects. Should you use a typewriter? How do you know where to send your stories? How much postage should you put on the envelope? What if they steal your idea? Fee of $15.00 for professor to read and evaluate each student paper.

LAMBERT GLIBB

MC/#5:
REMEDIAL TELEVISION

Course specially designed for students whose parents didn't let them watch TV, thereby alienating them from modern American culture. Divided into segments on variety shows, situation comedies, Saturday morning cartoons, adventure series, and specials. (Shows appearing on Public Television will be discussed in Mass Communications/1066, Highbrow Media.)

FRANK LLOYD KOVALCHICK

MATHEMATICS

Not a day goes by when we don't all have to deal with numbers in one way or another. Some people, in fact, prefer to communicate with numbers rather than with words or people. Most of them end up as math majors. Department Chairman Procter Gamble exemplifies math majors' preference for real numbers over the real world. The beauty and clarity of the fundamental concepts make remoteness from the hazy subjectivity of verbal thought even more desirable. Most students are grateful for the physical isolation of the Fernquist Math Center, with its calculators, computers, and oversized chess boards, and it is usually filled to capacity during the peak hours between 8 P.M. and 6 A.M. At any time of night, packs of math majors can be seen chuckling and gossiping about the latest logarithmic equations while buying sodas and snacks from the competing private concession stands run by enterprising business majors in the Math Center. Graduates from this department can look forward to careers in teaching high school or in government service in offices decorated with green linoleum.

Requirements for the Major:
Students must be able to program binomial functions on a hand-held calculator in the dark and to multiply in their heads. To determine class standing at the end of senior year, students compete in Prof. Procter Gamble's Math Olympics. Events include: moving decimals, map coloring, plot-

ting graphs, carrying over the variable, and two-person zero sum games. NOTE: Although mathematics is the universal language, majors should be reminded that it does not fulfill the foreign language requirement.

MATH/409:
DULL NORMAL MATHEMATICS

For students who do not have a firm grasp of high school mathematics and will need some elementary mathematical techniques in later courses, and later life for that matter. A terminal course for students not intending to continue the study of mathematics and who probably couldn't even if they wanted to. *This course does not carry credit toward the bachelor's degree!* The Help Room on the 6th Floor of the Fernquist Math Center is open to students seeking individual help from the instructors and teaching assistants occasionally present. Videotape equipment is also available for problem solving and recreation.

PROCTER GAMBLE

MATH/1066:
INTRODUCTION TO DISCREET MATHEMATICS

How to estimate a restaurant bill before it arrives. Calculating tips for taxis and bellhops. Guessing prices in fancy stores where they don't use price tags. Gauging appropriate expenditure for gifts. Estimating sales tax and shipping charges. Special attention will be paid to foreign currency exchange and VAT.

LORD PENNYLACKING

MATH/π–1:
FUNDAMENTAL ALGORITHMS

Pattern matching, backtracking, fox trotting, divide and conquer, live and let live, do or die, now or never, graph searching, finding patterns in strings, spanning trees, balanced trees, B-trees, 2-3 trees, C3PO trees, spraying trees for caterpillars. Other topics as time permits. Field trips to Candlewood State Park.

IRVING KLUPFERBERG

Audiovisual aids make math classes easy and fun.

PHOTO BUG

MATHEMATICS IN THE REAL WORLD

Not offered this year.

MATH/1776:
UNSOLVED PROBLEMS

Squaring the circle, the Bermuda Triangle, balancing the federal budget, getting blood stains out of carpet, losing weight without dieting. Some knowledge of mathematics would be helpful but is not essential.

KINGSTON MILDEW

MATH/#5:
MODEL THEORY

This course concentrates on the relative figures of modeling—salaries, measurements, agency fees, success/failure ratios, percentage deals on product endorsements, etc. Attention will be paid to the careers of Shelley Hack, Cheryl Tiegs, Cybill Shepherd, Sherry Lansing, Suzy Parker, and Brooke Shields. Prerequisite: Students must submit portfolios.

FRANK LLOYD KOVALCHICK

MATH/4 to 6:
MEET THE INTEGERS

Students are introduced to 1, 2, 3, 4, 5, 6, 7, 8, 9, 10.

MRS. ROGERS

MATH/12 oz.:
PROBABILITY

The effect of carrying an umbrella on the chances it will rain. Choosing lanes in a traffic jam or at the supermarket. Some attention will be paid to romantic questions and the odds against finding a suitable mate. Games of chance will be covered in detail.

DOWNING BEERY

MATH/π-2:
CALCULUS

This course is intended for students who have had enough calculus to be able to differentiate between polynomial and bodily functions and would like to concentrate on their preference.

IRVING KLUPFERBERG

MATH/1,000 V:
LOGIC

The work of this course is directed toward the understanding of logical concepts like proof, validity, consistency, and hearsay. *This course is required for all math majors.* Prerequisite: Students are required to demonstrate proficiency by passing an entrance exam. Passing grade on the exam automatically exempts student from the course but no credit will be given.

NORMAN BATES

MATH/III:
GASTRONOMICAL GEOMETRY

The shapes of eggs, vegetables, and other ingredients; building foods; cake pans, their shapes and sizes; measurement of edible surfaces; slicing for accurate portion control. Course project includes construction and consumption of a wedding cake.
(Also HE/III-6)

H.A.G. KLUMPP

MATH/$3:
HOMOLOGICAL ALGEBRA

Students examine pertinent questions as:
    Q.: How many gays does it take to screw in a light bulb?
    A.: Two: one to put it in and another to scream "Fabulous!"

REV. BRUCE CADEMYTE

MUSIC

In the words of a famous British writer, music has charms to soothe the savage breast, which explains the large percentage of buxom women majors enrolled in the Music Department. Like many of the academic departments at Mount Merry, the Music Department places its main emphasis on the everyday applications of the material under study. Specifically, this means students develop an appreciation of everything from the value of a good car radio on long trips to the artistic serviceability of the kazoo. Secondly, the department is highly responsive to student interest, which means that modern and popular music is its main focus. LeRoi Paxton, the department chairman, has a native aptitude for popular musical forms of the latter half of this century. As a working musician himself, he brings a heightened sensitivity to the problems of performance and sound systems. In his career, he has devoted study to a broad range of aural concerns including tonal awareness, harmonic complexity, and loud plaid jackets.

Due to the department's extensive coverage of jazz, rock'n'roll, and disco, large record store chains regularly recruit majors as salesmen. Other majors who study performance have gone on to highly visible careers as street musicians in Waterbury or as members of Guy Lombardo's Royal Canadians.

Requirements for the Major:

The primary emphasis is on listening rather than performing, but any sort of musical activity which enlarges listening pleasure is recognized as an advantage, so students must develop proficiency at whistling, singing along in harmony, and playing percussion on any available surface, resonant or nonresonant. Within the department, students may elect to follow Program I (highbrow music) or Program II (fun music). It should be noted that Program I, kindly administered by Dr. Mildew, has been cancelled in recent years due to insufficient interest.

MUS/33⅓–1:
FUNDAMENTALS OF JAZZ

This course will cover advanced concepts of jazz. Students will learn that you gotta suffer to sing the blues, t'ain't what you do it's the way that you do it, and it don't mean a thing if it ain't got that swing. Class project: Students must build a stairway to the stars.

LeRoi Paxton

MUS/100G's:
POPULAR SONGWRITING AND ARRANGEMENT

The art, technique, and science of writing popular songs. Representative examples from the prom, the rock palace, the jukebox, and the car radio will be studied. Students will study words that rhyme with "love," "romance," and "kiss." Guest lecturers may include Barry Manilow, Marvin Hamlisch, and Neil Diamond. Recommended for guys who were ugly and unpopular in high school. Ability to play musical instrument or read music helpful but by no means essential.

Lambert Glibb

MUS/33⅓–2:
RHYTHM

An investigation into a natural phenomenon. Students are instructed in the dynamics of finger snapping, toe tapping, head nodding, and clapping. This course is recommended for students who can't sit still when they hear the Motown sound.

LeRoi Paxton

MUS/12 oz.:
MUSIC IN WHITE AMERICAN CULTURE

White music from its European origins to the various forms in which it exists in America today. Tradition of the ballad, marches, and dance music as interpreted by Lawrence Welk, the Andrews Sisters, Robert Goulet, Arthur Fiedler, Anne Murray, and Debbie Boone. Hits include "Smoke Gets In Your Eyes," "Raindrops Keep Fallin' On My Head," "Tomorrow," "The Way We Were," and "Feelings."

Downing Beery

MUS/1776–1:
MASTERPIECES

An intensive listening course which enables students to sound educated about classical music. Key passages and their uses as themes in modern film and television are drilled into students' memories until they are immediately recognizable. Among the works studied are: Beethoven's Ninth Symphony, Chorale Movement; Mozart's Twenty-First Piano Concerto in C major (K. 467); Vivaldi's "The Four Seasons," "Spring"; Chopin's Nocturnes, No. 1 in B flat minor (op. 9 No. 1); Brahms's "Lullaby," and any of J. S. Bach's Brandenburg Concertos. Required listening: Kingston Mildew's "Masterpieces of Classical Music" radio show on WONK from 2:00 A.M. to 6:00 A.M.

Kingston Mildew

MUS/90 lb.:
LISTENING TO MUSIC

Students are exposed to the fundamentals of listening to music; the on/off button, volume, and selection. Alternatives for music listening are considered, from the live variety to portable stereo units. Emphasis will be placed on special variations like car stereo, rock concerts, and roommates singing in the shower.

Caspar Q. Wimpley

MUS/747:
PROBLEMS IN
OPERA

Through study of plot and score, students explore some of the knotty questions of great operas. Do people always dress like that in cigar factories? Is there no cure for the consumption that carried off Mimi and Violetta? What makes a sustaining meal that won't put you to sleep between the acts of the *Ring* cycle? How could Tosca jump into the Tiber from the Castel Sant' Angelo when it's 1½ miles away?

PEPE LE PUE

MUS/#5:
POP MUZIK

Students talk about pop muzik, radio, video. You'll boogie with a suitcase, you'll be living in a disco, you'll forget about the rat race, so let's do the milkshake and hop like a hotcake, try some, buy some, fee, fi, fo, fum, talk about pop muzik, shoobedoobedoowop.

FRANK LLOYD KOVALCHICK

MUS/1776–2:
THE BACH FAMILY

A study in the foremost family in music, the Bachs. How did Johann Sebastian pass along his talents to Johann Christian, Wilhelm Friedemann, and Carl Philipp Emanuel? What kind of influence did Anna Magdalena have on the family business? Highlights: a measure-by-measure examination of the J.S. and C.P.E. Bach "Magnificats," and a refutation of the statement that "listening to Bach is like being hit on the head with a teaspoon."

KINGSTON MILDEW

MUS/40:
CHOIR

No audition necessary. Students learn by doing: following a conductor, carrying a tune, drowning out your tone-deaf neighbor, turning pages without making a lot of noise, getting your robe on right. Performance at Sunday morning services. May be repeated for credit (extra credit for real singers). Repertoire does not include secular hits.

REV. MOSES SAVONAROLA

PHILOSOPHY

Man has questioned his very existence ever since his creation or evolution (that's a philosophical question right there). Man has always asked himself: Why am I here? Why do I feel and think? Why must I do? Why am I always talking to myself?

The Philosophy Department at Mount Merry takes a radical approach to these questions. As its dynamic department chairman Bruno Coxman puts it, a mere smattering of philosophical history shows that philosophers are constantly changing their minds. First one, then another, then yet another system of thought is in fashion. Obviously, claims Prof. Coxman, they have all been wrong about some things. The thesis of Mount Merry's department is that, at its best, philosophy helps men decide how to run their lives and this is the major focus of the course offerings. By taking a sampling of courses, students have a wide selection of philosophies to choose from. Students are invited to try a number of them out and, by graduation, to pick the one that best complements their personalities. Grades will be awarded on the basis of the appropriateness of students' selections and the consistency with which they have carried them out.

Requirements for the Major:

Requirements in the department are based more on imagination than on academic performance, since students are expected to subscribe wholeheartedly to the tenets, major and minor, of any philosophy they are studying. For this reason, if two departmental courses are to be taken in a semester, they should be compatible, i.e., Platonic Philosophy (PHIL/40–2) and Ethics (PHIL/40–1), or Epicureanism (PHIL/#5–2) and Playboy Philosophy (PHIL/8″). Students must choose a final life philosophy by midsemester senior year, and as a project, prepare a Life Brief which demonstrates in detail how they will meet the future. Periodic postgraduate reports to the departmental chairman are expected for the following ten years. Failure to report will result in the revocation of the diploma.

PHIL/280Z–1:
INTRODUCTION TO
PHILOSOPHICAL THEORY

Empiricism, ontology, epistemology, gnoseology—their application, pronunciation, and how to tell them apart.

DOO WOP

PHIL/8″:
THE PLAYBOY PHILOSOPHY

What sort of student takes this course? A student with a lust for life who wants the best that life can give. Students are encouraged to act cool, pretend they know a lot about wine, cars, clothes, and stereos. Homework includes varied and intensive sexual activity with class reports the next day. Heightening the material is certainly allowed. Final exam: comprehensive review of party jokes. Required text: *Unabashed Dictionary*.

BRUNO COXMAN

PHIL/1776:
CONCEPTS OF EXISTENCE

Questions of being and presence are explored as students are asked to decide if they really exist. Emphasis will be placed on existential ultra-ideologies created in response to the upsetting shifts triggered by modernity and its technological advances: hologram, photograph, or real person? Is it live or is it Memorex? Class attendance optional, since it can be argued that presence is relative.

KINGSTON MILDEW

PHIL/#5-1:
AESTHETICS

This course will explore the central questions of aesthetics, viz.: What is the relation between the work of art, the creative act, the viewer's experience, the socio-historical world in which they are embedded, and what the artist thought of his mother? Knowledge of art is unnecessary; knowledge of what you like, essential.

FRANK LLOYD KOVALCHICK

PHIL/40-2:
PLATONIC PHILOSOPHY

Why not to sleep with people; how to keep a friendship clean. Selected readings from Plato, St. Augustine, St. Paul, John Calvin, and Pope John Paul II. Topics covered include cold showers, jogging, saltpeter, and the risk of touch dancing. Students must enroll in couples.

REV. MOSES SAVONAROLA

PHIL/#5-2:
EPICUREANISM

Why living well is the best revenge, and key techniques for doing so. Students learn about fast cars, Italian leathers, European luxury hotels, and fresh flowers on a daily basis. The main stress of the course is laid on the pleasures of the table, including oysters, foie gras, and vintage Burgundies. Some attention will be paid to digestion and financing techniques.

FRANK LLOYD KOVALCHICK

PHIL/19th:
LANGUAGE AND INTERPRETATION

This course explores mutually informing modes of articulation throughout human experience. Emphasis will be placed on interpretation of every linguistic transaction, save those exchanged under conditions of complete conventionality. Semiotics, semantics, little white lies, truth and translation, viz.: "Your check is in the mail," "I'll call you tomorrow," and "Trust me, I'll stop in time."

NATASHA GOLDMAN

PHIL/280Z-2:
EASTERN PHILOSOPHY

Confucius say: Good fortune will be yours. Follow the straight road to success. Your personality is your coat of armor. Beware of a dark handsome stranger. The moon is smiling on your future. Put up with small annoyances to gain great results. And more. Students must bring own fortune cookies.

DOO WOP

PHIL/40-1:
ETHICS

Some theories of morality and value: free will, absolutism and relativism, egoism and altruism. Situation ethics in contemporary life, such as bank errors in your favor, infidelity, cheating at solitaire, and broaching the topic of birth control on a date. Readings to include David Hume, Emmanuel Kant, and Emily Post.

REV. MOSES SAVONAROLA

PHIL/747:
CONTINENTAL PHILOSOPHY

What are they thinking on the continent? *Idées reçues* and the classic *Weltanschauung*, as well as current attitudes toward life as influenced by the tourist season and the trends at the current Cannes Film Festival. Students may choose from workshops investigating regional cuisine, fashion, dance styles, and notions of modesty in bathing suits.

PEPE LE PUE

PHIL/$3:
GREEK PHILOSOPHY

An appreciation of Socrates, Plato, Demosthenes, Epicurus, their teachings, practices, pederasty, with special emphasis on the weekend action at the Lyceum.

REV. BRUCE CADEMYTE

PHYSICAL EDUCATION

Physical education is very important at Mount Merry, as evinced by the unusual four-year physical education requirement that insists that all Mount Merry students participate in some regular physical activity during their years at the college. The academic department of physical education, however, should not be confused with the extracurricular activities. Based on the assumption that good sportsmanship fosters good citizenship, the department offers a full major, above and beyond playing organized sports for "fun."

The physical education major, according to the department's able and enthusiastic Co-chairperson (female) Mary Dyche, is intended either for students who plan to make their careers in the field of physical education, or for students who would like to avoid contact with books. Prof. Dyche's colleague, Co-chairperson (male) Steve E. Dore (affectionately known as "Moose"), when asked to expand on the department's outlook, responded, "Yes."

Requirements for the Major:

An interview with the Department Co-chairperson (female) is required, during which students are expected to demonstrate their fitness in a series of tests devised by Professor Dyche. Criteria for fitness include muscular strength, flexibility, sports skills, and, above all, stamina. These will be judged impartially by her. Once accepted as majors, students must take a minimum of eight credits in physical education courses. There is no maximum. Many courses may be repeated for credit, and independent study is encouraged. Recent semester-long projects approved by Professor Dyche have been "Pain and Fitness" and "The Effect of Bilateral Injury on Coordination." Mr. Dore has supervised projects in "Fencing Alone" and "Sports Without Balls."

PE/CT5334-62-78-1:
SPORT STRATEGIES AND TECHNIQUES

The concentration in this course is on the mechanical analysis of intimidating the opponent. Such methods as verbal harassment, tripping, fisticuffs, and Ben-Gay ointment surreptitiously slathered on jock straps will be reviewed. Essays on good sportsmanship by John McEnroe, Muhammad Ali, and Bear Bryant are included among the required texts.

LEON DE THUGG

PE/90 lb.:
FIRST AID

Standard procedures of administering first aid: how to peel open a bandage, reading the label first, remembering the emergency number to the hospital. This course is required for all who enroll in Sport Strategies and Techniques; Self-Defense; Action Speaks Louder Than Words; Residual Effects of Alcohol on the Human Body; Body Building and Slenderizing, and Latin American Social Dancing.

CASPAR Q. WIMPLEY

PE/38D-2:
BODY BUILDING AND SLENDERIZING

Working with weights to make your body look the way you want it to. A rigorous series of exercises will be followed. Even the biggest challenges are welcomed. The instructor reserves the right to impose a stricter and harsher regimen, if necessary.

MARY DYCHE

PE/12 oz.:
RESIDUAL EFFECTS OF ALCOHOL ON THE HUMAN BODY

How to function despite a hangover. Is whiskey really the safest liquor? Does it help to drink milk beforehand? Does aspirin *before* you go to sleep make a difference? Do prairie oysters really work? Causes, cures, and preventions: the whirlies, mixing liquors in your stomach. Special night workshop/labs. Lab fee: BYOB.

DOWNING BEERY

PE/CT5334–62–78–2:
SELF-DEFENSE

Useful techniques for theoretical and practical application, including the principles of evasion, concealment, and attack. Preliminary bout with instructor required. To be taken in conjunction with "Health and Convalescence" (not offered this year).

LEON DE THUGG

PE/38D–1:
THEORIES IN PHYSICAL EDUCATION

The components of fitness and achieving them, expressed in the writings and lives of Charles Atlas, Johnny Weissmuller, Marjorie Craig, and Suzy Prudden. NOTE: Although this is a theory course consisting of two weekly lectures and demonstrations enacted by students, it does not satisfy the extracurricular physical education requirement.

MARY DYCHE

PE/00–4:
SLEEP AND FITNESS

We will examine the need for sleep and its effect on performance. Topics include: dream patterns, rapid eye movement, sleeping around vs. sleeping alone, and whether or not to wear pajamas in hot weather. Attention will also be paid to sleeping position, naps, and narcotics.

STEVE E. DORE

PE/CT5334–62–78–3:
ACTION SPEAKS LOUDER THAN WORDS

(See SP/CT5334–62–78)

PE/00–1:
HEALTH AND HYGIENE

Introduction to the habits of good hygiene. Students find out what a toothbrush is for, discuss brand recognition in deodorant and soap, and learn the advisability of flossing on a daily basis. Also stressed are basic hair care and combating acne with over-the-counter preparations.

STEVE E. DORE

PE/00–2:
ATHLETIC OFFICIATING I

Training in the techniques of refereeing and/or umpiring football, basketball, baseball, track, and tennis. Keeping all the hand signals straight, blowing the whistle, and staying out of the way. Some time will be spent on the psychological implications of being hated by a crowd.

STEVE E. DORE

PE/00–3:
ATHLETIC OFFICIATING II

Advanced training in refereeing and umpiring, involving more complex problems, viz.: crew (how not to get seasick), ice hockey (avoiding the sticks and blades), rugby (staying out of the scrum), and polo (staying on the horse). When possible, students will officiate at intramural events (horses not included).

STEVE E. DORE

PE/38D–3:
LATIN AMERICAN SOCIAL DANCING

Rumba, cha-cha, tango, Latin hustle. Attention is focused on choice of music, costume, and partner. Also available as independent study.

MARY DYCHE

PHYSICS

The science of physics attempts to examine the laws governing the physical world: matter, movement, light, and other spooky subjects. It usually requires a degree of mathematical skill or competency and a capacity to deal with abstracts, like particles so small you can't even see them, the space-time continuum, and sound as little wavy squiggles in the air. Although physics does not allow you to mess around with test tubes, crucibles, and animal corpses, students do get a chance to play with magnets, compasses, and other toys while wearing white lab coats.

Under the able guidance of its chairman, Joe Franklin, the Physics Department at Mount Merry is made more accessible to the capabilities of our students and is brought into reference with the domestic world. By applying physical principles to their bodies and some small electric appliances, students can call themselves physics majors. While this department does not prepare students for graduate work in physics, many of them have gone on to distinguished careers as mechanics. (An astute coordination of courses in the Physics and Foreign Languages Departments, for instance, could lay the groundwork for a specialist in foreign sports cars.)

Requirements for the Major:
All Physics majors must take Statistical Physics (PHYπ-1) or demonstrate that they will never in their natural lives need the information imparted in that course. An impressive collection of autographed photographs of stars may qualify students for advanced standing in astronomy.
Majors must return lab coats at the end of the school term.

PHY/CT5334-62-78:
MECHANICS
A study of Newton's laws, the conservation laws of classical mechanics, and their application to physical systems—carburetors, batteries, transmissions, and spark plugs. One hour lecture, three hour lab in body shop. Experimental material will be drawn from faculty parking lot.

LEON DE THUGG

PHY/2 am:
DESCRIPTIVE ASTRONOMY
General knowledge of the facts of astronomy and investigation of the life span of a star: starlet, promising newcomer, major talent, bankable star, industry spokesman, has-been. Basic texts: Norman Mailer's *Marilyn*, Richard Schickel's *The Stars*, and the writings of Rex Reed.

JOE FRANKLIN

PHY/12 oz.:
PHYSICS FOR DILETTANTES
This course is for the technically uninformed student who wants to glimpse science in the modern world. Theories of energy and relativity will be discussed. In doing so, as much, if not more, emphasis will be placed on the scientist as on the science—the class's celebration of Einstein's birthday has become legend. A second aspect of the course is to introduce the student to some of the ways in which science influences and affects society—you'd be surprised.

DOWNING BEERY

PHY/$3:
FLUIDS, WAVES AND HEAT
An introductory study of fluid mechanics, characteristics in elastic media, and basic thermal phenomena in commonly encountered manifestations. The course will examine saunas, hot tubs, Jacuzzis, and steam baths. Prerequisite: a towel and a bathing suit.

REV. BRUCE CADEMYTE

PHY/100%:
ATOMIC AND NUCLEAR PHYSICS
The experimental basis of modern atomic and nuclear physics with a concentration on the foremost topics of modern science—the development of the atomic bomb and nuclear reactors. The principles of their component and system design as well as operating characteristics are the primary focus. Students construct the power system of their choice and negotiate its sale to third world countries.

HUGO MARKUP

PHY/90 lb.:
FUNDAMENTALS OF LABORATORY MEASUREMENT
Experiments selected to demonstrate the use of slide rules, thermometers, compasses, yardsticks, etc. Prerequisite: charge account at student store.

CASPAR Q. WIMPLEY

PHY/π-2:
ELECTRONICS
This course covers the review of the basic laws of electrical currents, detection instruments, power sources, amplifiers, recorders, synthesizers, turntables, receivers, disco mixers. Students learn to evaluate fidelity and volume of sound systems on a 45–90 scale based on a good beat, "easy to dance to" quotient, and whether they would buy it themselves.

IRVING KLUPFERBERG

PHY/III:
MICROWAVE STUDIES
An examination of the microwave and its applications in the kitchen. Thawing, roasting, and broiling; the containers to use for best results; and innovative applications. (Warning: The microwave is not recommended for grooming of pets.)
(Also Home Economics HE/III-5)

H.A.G. KLUMPP

PHY/π-1:
STATISTICAL PHYSICS
The treatment, by concept and method, of systems made up of very many particles. Application to superconductivity, superfluidity, superfluity, elementary transport phenomena, and black body radiation. Required for satisfaction of Physics Department requirements. May be repeated until passing grade achieved.

IRVING KLUPFERBERG

PHY/00:
GIANTS OF PHYSICAL THOUGHT

An introduction to the writings of physical thinkers such as Newton, Lagrange, Maxwell, Fourier, and Schwarzenegger. When possible, experiments will relate to topics under study. Some change in musculature may be noted.

STEVE E. DORE

POLITICS

When a group of two or more people get together, somebody's got to be in charge, and Department Chairman Colonel Ulysses S. Hawk prefers it to be himself. The study of politics concerns the process by which some people always seem to end up running other people's lives. At Mount Merry, the Politics Department specifically examines the secondary notions of ideology, government techniques, law and courts, and cooperation between political systems. However, the central focus of the Politics Department is the question of power. Who has it? Where does it come from? Can it be bought? Is it animal, vegetable, mineral? Or none of the above?

Although the department offers courses on a national and international scale, the most popular courses discuss the power structure at Mount Merry itself. These special year-long colloquia, which meet in biweekly sessions, have generated word-of-mouth interest for their realistic evaluation of the personalities and dynamics that run Mount Merry. Though these colloquia are open to all students, politics majors are strongly urged to sign up for them early to reserve a place, owing to their overwhelming popularity. Topics of these sessions include: "Sex in the Administration" (Coxman and Feeley)—What really went on between Dr. Kaiser and ex-Carrie Nation Temperance College Headmistress Mildred Maim? What do you think The O'Kays do out there on that farm with Gretchen Indigo?; "The Power of Economics" (Shyster)—If the alumni dormitory fund drive fell so abysmally short, then how come the new upperclass women's dorm is so luxurious?; and "The Case for Physical Discipline" (Dyche)—How Rolfing could straighten that Harry Palmer out.

Requirements for the Major:

Although class work is certainly germane to the course of study, independent work plays a decisive role in the students' development. Majors plan, organize, and manipulate all student government events and elections. They choose to run for office, to play a backstage role in the election, or simply to donate a large sum to the campaign and be appointed ambassador to Luxembourg. This system gives politics majors invaluable experience in campaigning, press relations, responsiveness to the electorate, and cosmetic concerns like makeup and hair dye. Elections are held on a yearly basis; terms are restricted to two years. The losers of each election forfeit the privilege of being politics majors and are required to transfer to the History Department where Dr. Mildew will welcome them.

POL/1066:
EUROPEAN POLITICS AND DIPLOMACY

An introduction to cultural approaches to individual European countries. The effect of the international political structure on the American abroad. Topics will include: handy foreign phrases, ordering from a native menu, asking directions, and hygiene habits. Recommended for students planning to study abroad.

LORD PENNYLACKING

POL/280Z-2:
LEFT, RIGHT, AND CENTER

A survey of contemporary currents of American political thought such as the "counter culture," the new left, the new right, liberalism, conservatism, and straddling the fence-ism. Students are asked to distinguish each from the other.

DOO WOP

POL/14th:
INTEREST GROUPS, LOBBYING, AND THE POLITICAL PROCESS

This course analyzes the practical realities of pressure groups and lobbying in Washington. A special emphasis will be placed on the resources and tactics of successful lobbyists. A field trip to Washington will be held at the end of the semester so that students may witness this process in action as they lobby for an increase in federal funding of higher education.

DAISY McGILLICUDDY

POL/280Z-1:
FROM MARX TO MAO

An examination of viable alternative ideologies and how they could conceivably be applied to the American political scene. Texts include *The Communist Manifesto* and *Sayings of Chairman Mao*. Students learn to construct Molotov cocktails and pipe bombs.

Doo Wop

POL/1776:
PRESIDENTS

The leaders of our country; how to identify them, what made them great. Special emphasis is placed on such forgotten figures as Millard Fillmore, James Polk, Warren Harding, Rutherford B. Hayes, Martin van Buren, John Garfield, and Richard Nixon. The dynamics of public opinion will be tested by special polls in the Waterbury area.

Kingston Mildew

POL/19th:
INTRODUCTION TO AMERICAN POLITICS

The political process in our country—the rights and responsibilities of each citizen. The main goal of the course will be to equip students for an intelligent reading of the *Washington Post*. Some attention will be paid to the important roles of blonde TV newscasters and gossip columnists.

Natasha Goldman

POL/1967:
INTERNATIONAL RELATIONS

The advantages and drawbacks of having relatives in the Old Country. Keeping in touch so you can stay with them when abroad: aerogram technique, keeping up with phone rates, inexpensive gifts that won't break in the mail. Attention will be paid to losing your accent without offending your grandmother.

Gretchen Indigo

POL/B-52:
LATIN AMERICAN POLITICS

An examination of the patterns and theories of Latin American political movements. How to tell the good guys from the bad guys, i.e., which side the United States is funding. We will use as primary text the book and lyrics for *Evita*, with further attention paid to the lives of Bianca Jagger, Carmen Miranda, and Ricardo Montalban.

Col. Ulysses Hawk

PSYCHOLOGY

Psychology is essentially examination of behavior; the things people do, why they do them, what they mean. Students of psychology gain an acute awareness of personal dynamics in their relationships in and out of the classroom, and some even claim that they are better programmed to get what they want.

Mount Merry's Psychology Department recognizes that study of its subject must not be limited to theory or experimentation, but must also examine the psychological experience *as it occurs*. To this end, students participate in weekly encounter sessions with Department Chairman Norman Bates and other members of the faculty. (A notarized parental release for students under twenty-one is necessary.) Most students regard these encounter sessions as one of the high points of the psychology curriculum, citing the work they do that applies to courses such as Sensations (PSY/$69 + 8''$–2), States of Consciousness (PSY/250mg), and Self-Abuse (PSY/1). "I always feel great after my encounter sessions," students say again and again and again.

Departmental students may choose to follow either Track 1 or Track 2 in their course work. Track 1 students are advised by Professor Rush of the Chemistry Department, and concentrate on the mechanical workings of the brain as they are affected by man-made substances. Students planning to be pharmacists or narcotics agents may find this career preparation especially helpful. Track 2 focuses on the interaction between the sexes, especially on an intimate, one-on-one basis. Professors Feeley, Coxman, Rev. Cademyte, and, occasionally, Professor Palmer lend a hand to counsel Track 2 students. Mount Merry graduates claim to have found this course of study helpful and liberating, no matter what their walk of life.

Professor Bates administers, with the cooperation of the Sociology Department, a program in Deviant Studies, his specialty. In addition to Social Deviants (PSY/1,000 V–1) and Deviance and Social Control (SOC/409), independent field work is undertaken with Professor Bates's guidance. To insure sufficient variety of study subjects, this work usually requires a term's residence in New York City.

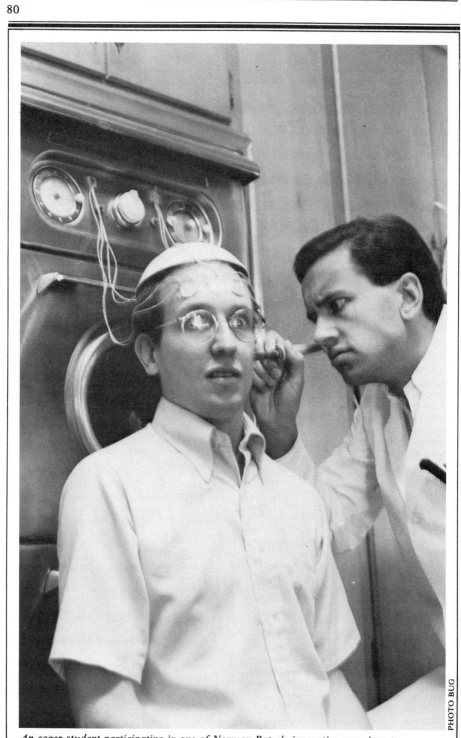

PHOTO BUG

An eager student participating in one of Norman Bates's innovative experiments.

Requirements for the Major:

The Psychology Department lays great stress on the techniques of experimental psychology, and each student must accumulate at least three terms' credit for lab work. At least one of these terms must be in the capacity of a volunteer, preferably the final term of senior year. (Diplomas will be awarded regardless of students' state at year's end.) Negotiations with School Comptroller Izzy A. Shyster and provision of experimental animals (300 rats, for example, or a truckload of chickens) occasionally result in an exemption from the volunteer requirement.

In addition, psychology majors take turns staffing the Psychological Studies Center on campus, which runs a suicide hotline and offers counseling hours for disturbed students, faculty members, and residents of Waterbury. Since a fresh approach, undiluted by experience, is desirable, PsychoCenter staffing experience should begin sophomore year.

PSY/1776 + 1,000 V-2:
DREAM ANALYSIS

The psychology of dreams is investigated—the sleep-dream process, dream recall, and theories on the meaning of dreams—by practical methods. Class begins with a fifteen-minute lecture by Dr. Mildew on the history of oneirocritical literature, followed by Professor Bates's wiring of the slumbering students for his own analytic purposes.

NORMAN BATES AND KINGSTON MILDEW

PSY/8"-3:
APPLIED SEXUALITY (formerly URBAN AFFAIRS)

Theories and practice of the mechanical nature of sex will be explored as students visit a number of houses of ill repute in Waterbury. Prerequisite: Students must undergo physicals before and after each class. Lab Fee: Pay as you go.

BRUNO COXMAN

PSY/250mg:
STATES OF CONSCIOUSNESS

Sleeping, dreaming, arousal, attention, and altered cognitive states are all measured in class. The investigation and interpretation of dreams by Freud and other psychoanalysts, and more recent chemical techniques. The functions and processes underlying consciousness, such as drug-induced conditions and hallucinating, are compared with dreams and attentive consciousness, both as phenomena and pleasurable experiences. Lab Fee: current market rate.

ROB RUSH

PSY/1,000 V-1:
SOCIAL DEVIANTS

An investigation of various modes of behavior and social expectations. Why don't some people fit in? Why are they always causing trouble? What should society do about them? This course applies a Hobbesian approach to the psychological problems of the aberrant. Class attendance mandatory or else.

NORMAN BATES

PSY/4 to 6:
PSYCHOLOGICAL TESTING

What do psychological tests really measure? How are they scored? Are the people who grade them really so smart? The goal of this course is to enable students to achieve the results they want on tests for the purposes of gaining employment or avoiding the draft. What is the significance of seeing only phalluses in Rorschach samples? Who cares which picture is different? What does that have to do with earning potential? Can you place below (or above, if need be) "dull normal" in an IQ test? How can you tell when you're being given a test? All results will be kept strictly confidential.

MRS. ROGERS

PSY/PSY:
WHAT'S YOUR PROBLEM?

Find it hard to get a date? Do you worry about your own mortality? Do you have difficulty with bad breath? See things out of the corner of your eye—that aren't there? Are you being followed? Do you have an invisible "friend"? Can you fly? Do you love your father? Your mother? Students investigate their own neuroses under expert guidance. Lab Fee: $80.00/hour; each hour consists of 50 minutes.

DR. ALEXANDER LUCRE

PSY/1776:
ADULTHOOD AND AGING

The implications of becoming "mature," and some approaches to the problems of aging—going grey and going bald, crow's feet, liver spots, weight gain. Professor Mildew, from his own extensive experience, pontificates on why it's better to face up to them. How Grecian Formula really works. Why you are never too old for a face-lift. Whether you should take out your dentures on a first date. Planning a wardrobe around spreading hips, for both men and women. The final class answers the question "Is there sex after sixty?" for the professor's benefit.

KINGSTON MILDEW

PSY/69 + 8"-1:
PERSONALITY AND SOCIAL RELATIONS

The components of personality and how they affect the ways others perceive us. What it means to be a good listener. When not to mention politics. How to talk about almost anything. What are some of the ways to show someone you like them? How can you use your voice and facial expressions to get your message across? What do certain gestures mean? Laboratory includes sessions at cocktail parties, in restaurants, on dance floors, and on couches. Credit will be arranged according to performance.

IRMA FEELEY and BRUCE COXMAN

PSY/69 + 8"-2:
SENSATIONS

An intimate inquiry into the senses. Care will be taken to refine and heighten the stimulation of all *five* senses. The course is structured to concentrate on each sense singly, then in combinations when the interactions of sensual perceptions are touched on. Though lingering attention will be focused on specific areas of stimulation, the course will build to a climax which includes all of the senses, and then some. Prerequisite: Personality and Social Relations (PSY/69 + 8"-1). Credit will be granted according to performance and based on a sliding scale.

IRMA FEELEY and BRUCE COXMAN

PSY/1:
SELF-ABUSE

What are the means by which we manipulate ourselves? Are you too hard on yourself? How do you handle yourself when the heat's on? A survey of the games people play with themselves, and ways of getting in touch. Class meets in informal "encounter" sessions.

HARRY PALMER

PSY/1,000 V-4:
MOTIVATION

Why do we do the things we do? Are there better reasons? Can we get other people to do what we want? Theories cover the gamut, from the carrot-on-a-stick to Jewish, Protestant, or Catholic guilt. We will examine in detail aspects of reward (money, power, sexual favors) and punishment (incarceration, physical correction, deprivation of favorite cookies).

NORMAN BATES

PSY/1,000 V-3:
PERCEPTION AND COGNITION

What was the name of your kindergarten teacher? What is on the second shelf of your refrigerator? How people answer these questions offers insight into human information processing. This course presents a clinical approach via experimentation beginning with rats and bunnies, and moving on to humans. (Students are expected to serve as subjects for at least one series of experiments.) Not for the squeamish.

NORMAN BATES

RELIGION AND THEOLOGY

Religion has been a guiding force in the development of arts and culture throughout the ages. A study of the historical and practical aspects of religious influences is beneficial to majors and non-majors alike because it provides a heightened imagination and sensitivity. This study is especially valuable preparation for the careers of evangelist, Christian housewife, and pornographer.

The legacy of Mount Merry Seminary lingers on at the college in more ways than just some of our more charming buildings or unusual disciplinary facilities. At Mount Merry, religion is a living concern, and nowhere is that more apparent than to the faculty of the Theology and Religion Department.

Though the department chairman, Reverend Savonarola, is a member of the Society of Jesus, the department does not devote more than ninety percent of syllabus time to the Judeo-Christian tradition. The special focus of the course offerings is the application of religion to life as we know it, in such crucial areas as the home, the office, and Hollywood.

Requirements for the Major:
Religion majors must take all of the courses offered in the department to demonstrate strength of purpose. Their private lives may also be subjected to scrutiny on an extracurricular basis, and commitment to the Religion Department does carry with it some limitations (for example, no religion major may register for a course taught by Professors Feeley, Coxman, Cademyte, or Palmer). Credit is given for singing in the choir and extra credit is awarded if you can carry a tune. Special arrangements may be made for such activities as visiting bordellos and bars with charity in mind.

Each student is required to do an independent study project in his senior year, either research or devotional in nature. Recent projects have included memorization of the entire Pentateuch, and construction of a diorama of the Last Supper.

REL/40-2:
THE GOSPEL ACCORDING TO HOLLYWOOD
An ecumenical survey of the various translations of Biblical stories from the Scriptures to the Silver Screen. How is adapting the Bible different from adapting other best sellers? Who is your favorite Christ—Ted Neeley, Max von Sydow, or Jeffrey Hunter? Students are asked to match Biblical characters with their Hollywood counterparts, e.g., Mary Magdalene—Carroll Baker. Prerequisite: Students must sit through *The Miracle of Our Lady of Fatima* in its entirety. This course is nondenominational.
REV. MOSES SAVONAROLA

REL/12 oz.:
RELIGIOUS STEREOTYPES
An investigation of the prevalent preconceptions about the major religions. Do WASP women really dislike sex? Are Catholic boys all repressed beyond repair? Why do Jewish women make love with their eyes closed? Class project will be the resolution of the following question: A Jew, a Catholic, and a Protestant jumped off the top of a building. Who landed first?
DOWNING BEERY

REL/1776:
LIFE IN THE MODERN CHURCH
An approach to man's role in the modern church. Should ladies still wear hats to services? Are gloves necessary? What about genuflection and crossing yourself? What are the proper conversational topics at the parish teas? What should you bake for the church bazaars? If you ask the priest to dinner, should you invite a single woman as well? What if the only single women you know are divorcées?
KINGSTON MILDEW

REL/19th-2:
HERMENEUTIC SEMANTICS
An introduction to religious reflection by analyzing the uses in modern Western culture of the words "know," "true," "mind," "person," "body," "love," "desire," "passion," "stop," "cut it out," "I mean it," "No!"
NATASHA GOLDMAN

REL/100%:
ETHICS AND THE PROFESSIONS
Classical ethical theories and secular and Judeo-Christian moral traditions as contexts for considering such moral problems as lying on your resumé, accepting kickbacks, prescribing ethical drugs unethically, performing unnecessary surgery, urging litigation when the client doesn't stand a chance, graft, embezzlement, and bribery. Recommended for business majors.
HUGO MARKUP

REL/19th-1:
"GOD": FACT OR FICTION?
A present-day look at the question of God and various ways of understanding the nature, if any, of divinity. Among the problems focused on will be: the Creation vs. evolution, the authorship of the Bible, the existence of evil, and why the New York Giants haven't won the championship since 1963.
NATASHA GOLDMAN

REL/50/50:
RELIGIOUS PERSONALITIES
A study of the lives and teachings of the paradigmatic figures of religions, both Christian and non-Christian. The course is divided between figures of the past (Moses, Jesus, Muhammad, Siddhartha) and the present (Jerry Falwell, Garner Ted Armstrong, Rev. Sun Myung Moon, Ernest Q. Ainslie, Guru Maharaj Ji, Billy Graham, Rex Humbard, and Rev. Ike), with emphasis on media techniques, diction, and hairstyle.
THE O'KAYS

Miss Irma Feeley's office door is always open.

REL/40–1:
GRACE AND SIN, PERSONAL AND SOCIETAL DIMENSIONS

Theology of grace in Scripture and in our personal and societal relationships. Students develop, through scrupulous self-examination, a keen sense of sin in everyday life. Special emphasis is placed on the Sixth through Tenth Commandments, and the mortal as opposed to venial sins. In special projects, students examine the manifestation and workings of the sin of their choice.

REV. MOSES SAVONAROLA

REL/III:
CHRISTIAN MARRIAGE AND FAMILY

Principles of marriage and family life according to Christian precepts. Stewardship of worldly goods, wholesome relations in the bedroom, family planning without contraception. Some questions taken up will be: how to protect children from the influence of television, how to think of interesting ways to eat fish every Friday, sharing the gospel with your neighbors, and Christian pets.

H.A.G. KLUMPP

SOCIOLOGY

Sociology involves the imposition of scientific method on the unscientific subject of people. By examining the individual and larger social units into which he may or may not fit, sociology proposes to tell man more about himself.

The Sociology Department at Mount Merry is particularly strong on the manifestation and treatment of antisocial behavior (a Deviant Social Studies Certificate is offered with the cooperation of the Psychology Department, under the expert guidance of Prof. Norman Bates), and on the dynamics of social stratification and class. For this reason, sociology is a recommended major for professional misfits, societal outcasts, gossip columnists, and gigolos.

Requirements for the Major
Majors in sociology are expected to take one course in each of the following areas: Theory and Methods, Social Institutions, the Individual and Family, and Comparative Sociology. If no course in one or more of these areas is offered during a student's years at Mount Merry, Lord Pennylacking, is willing to consider proposals for independent fulfillment of the requirements.

Though the Sociology Department does not require independent work, majors must take a comprehensive examination at the end of senior year, or, in a personal interview with Lord Pennylacking, convince him that they are above taking the exam. White gloves are suggested for the interview.

SOC/CT5334–62–78:
THE SOCIOLOGY OF IMPRISONMENT

An analysis of present patterns of incarceration and punishment in American society. Through student role-playing, the course will examine the relationships between the police, the judiciary, and the correctional system. The reality of prison life and prisoners' subcultures and rituals will be reenacted. Course will not appear on students' records.

LEON DE THUGG

SOC/1066–1:
SOCIAL INEQUALITY

A sociological salute to structured social inequality. Emphasis on the historical development of economic classes, status groups, and power elites, and the subversive organizations that would undermine them. Topics include: the nature of class (shabbygenteel vs. nouveau riche), methods of status-deprivation (replacing Gucci loafers with Thom McAnn's), the necessary role of bureaucracy in mediating conflict, maintaining social order, and stratifying neighborhoods. Social background required.

LORD PENNYLACKING

SOC/8″:
SEX STRATIFICATION AND THE SOCIAL EXPERIENCE OF MEN

The position of men in American society examined from the standpoints of role analysis and sexual expectation. Questions addressed include: Should you pretend to know more than you do? If you want to marry a virgin, how do you find one? How to tell if she's faking. How she can tell if you are. How to ask for what you really want in bed. How to deliver what she asks for. Theory and practice of opening lines and an investigation of the aphrodisiac controversy. Group discussion and relating of personal experience. Required reading: *Playboy*, *Hustler*, *The Sensuous Man*.

BRUNO COXMAN

SOC/π:
THE SOCIOLOGY OF THE POSSIBLE

Analysis of social thought about possible social arrangements—utopias, anti-utopias, and proposed social innovations—from Plato to writers of modern social science fiction, including the works of Andre Norton, Alan Dean Foster, Kenneth Robinson, and Boris Vallejo. Previous viewing of all episodes of "Star Trek" satisfies course requirements.

IRVING KLUPFERBERG

SOC/1066–2:
SOCIAL CHANGE IN CARIBBEAN SOCIETY

Examines social, political, and economic development and underdevelopment in the Caribbean. Have they caught on to the new, informal ways of entertaining? Do they know the new dances or are they still limited to the Limbo? Is it okay for a woman to ask a man over for a drink? When you dress for dinner, what do you *wear*?

LORD PENNYLACKING

SOC/B.C.:
OCCUPATIONS, PROFESSIONS, AND CAREERS

Examines the nature of the meaning of what people do all day. Occupational choices are considered, along with the learning of occupational roles, career mobility, and occupational lifestyles. Crafts, industrial and clerical, managerial and professional careers are the categories covered. Questions include why craftspeople wear sandals, why doctors play golf, and why businessmen always read the sports pages first.

EARL E. MANN

SOC/90 lb.:
RESEARCH METHODS

Analysis of strategies for discovery in social research, with emphasis on questionnaires, interviews, and observations. Students will apply these methods in a research project in Waterbury. Recent subjects have included examination of family hygiene habits, census of amphibian pets, and analysis of TV sitcom viewing. Fictional responses discouraged.

CASPAR Q. WIMPLEY

SOC/19th:
SOCIOLOGY AND THE FAMILY

We will attempt to answer these questions: How "natural" is the family institution? How essential is it? Are there better potential ways to get the housekeeping done? Analysis of cultural and religious context is considered desirable, but rarely achieved without extensive shouting.

NATASHA GOLDMAN

SOC/409:
DEVIANCE AND SOCIAL CONTROL

What constitutes social deviance? Must an act be considered "threatening" in order to qualify as deviance? Is body odor considered deviance? How about body odor in a small, enclosed space? Like an elevator—a *stuck* elevator? Can *any* antiperspirant keep it under control? Guest lecturer: Katie Winters.

PROCTER GAMBLE

SPEECH

The Speech Department aims to expose students to as wide a range of oral activity as is possible for their mouths to accommodate. This department differs from others in that it is inclined, not toward a vocational preparation, but rather toward personal gratification. Students may explore at leisure the full range of their special talents and interests, e.g., animal noises, scat singing, or yodeling. Majors study the human voice in an effort to see its relation to the process of oral communication. In order to master effective speaking, students learn how to inhale, exhale, resonate, articulate, and relax. Advanced students may also do all of the above while provocatively manipulating a cigarette.

Chairman Leon De Thugg contributes a special empathy for the needs of pre-articulate students in this field, as well as his personal brand of discipline and determination. Upon his suggestion, Action Speaks Louder Than Words (SP/CT5334–62–78) is compulsory, helping students to present their ideas and emotions in cogent and persuasive expression. Students are judged on individual performance, with emphasis on their ability to speak and listen effectively. Other courses stress training in the development of mental and emotional responsiveness to the meanings of words and other body noises. Chairman De Thugg's favorite field of study is debate, and his classroom tournaments inspire good attendance and heavy betting. Group Thinking and Discussion (SP/50/50) is offered for students who lack individual abilities in problem solving.

Requirements for the Major

Majors must take Action Speaks Louder than Words (SP/CT5334–62–78) and Oral Communication (SP/69+$3) under their choice of Irma Feeley or Rev. Bruce Cademyte. A special colloquium for majors on the techniques of Demosthenes must be preceded by mastery of the Heimlich maneuver. To graduate, students must write a speech entitled "What Mount Merry Means to Me," and deliver it in the Lucrezia Borgia Dining Hall during lunch. Final exam centers on complete recitation of the alphabet. Speech courses fulfill the foreign language requirement.

SP/CT5334–62–78:
ACTION SPEAKS LOUDER THAN WORDS

Using the body as an instrument of communication; special emphasis will be placed on obtaining satisfaction without recourse to speech, as well as knowing when to shut up and start punching.
(Also PE/CT5334–62–78–3)

LEON DE THUGG

SP/100G's:
ADVANCED PERSUASION

How to get what you want; psychology of intimidation, seduction, and winning delivery. Opportunities for field projects in a singles bar, obtaining a bank loan, returning merchandise to Woolworth's without a receipt.

LAMBERT GLIBB

SP/1066:
SMALL TALK

Acceptable topics for discussion in waiting rooms and at parties. Includes opening lines. Attention will be paid to the possibilities presented by the weather.

LORD PENNYLACKING

SP/50/50:
GROUP THINKING AND DISCUSSION

In this unstructured class, students choose a topic with the instructors and then discuss it at length. Past topics have included: fun beaches near Waterbury, comparative mileage of late model cars from Detroit, and fast and tasty sandwich ideas using Miracle Whip dressing.

THE O'KAYS

SP/4 to 6:
THE INTERROGATIVE MODE

Do you know how to ask a question? Can you believe there's a whole course on asking questions? Do you think that might be interesting?

MRS. ROGERS

SP/1,000 V:
GETTING RID OF YOUR ACCENT

Steps to clear, acceptable, unaffected speech through theory, practice, articulation, shock therapy. Labs take place in chapel; check hours. (Not to be taken if student has taken "English as a Foreign Language.")

NORMAN BATES

SP/90 lb.–1:
ENGLISH I

Sentences, asking questions, pronunciation, listening, grammar. Under the headings of pronunciation and listening are included: following directions, asking questions that verify the location of a place, person, or item.

CASPAR Q. WIMPLEY

SP/90 lb.–2:
THE ART OF THE SENTENCE

Students are trained to include predicates, nouns, pronouns in sentences. The second half of the semester deals with adverbs and adjectives, subordinate clauses, paragraphs, and verb tenses such as present and perfect.

CASPAR Q. WIMPLEY

SP/19th:
ARGUMENTATION

How to win arguments; talking back to your parents and other authority figures. Including epithets and breath control for maximum volume. Students will be encouraged to practice conversing with techniques like role playing and games.

NATASHA GOLDMAN

SP/69+$3:
ORAL COMMUNICATION

How to get results with your mouth—the function and purpose of oral communication, with analysis of individual performance. The instructors supervise the development of oral technique in each student for most effective results.

IRMA FEELEY or REV. BRUCE CADEMYTE

THE REUBEN DINGLEBERRY RANOLOGY INSTITUTE

The Institute for Ranology Studies was instituted in 1961 when alumnus Reuben Dingleberry ('14) generously donated $8 million for the construction of the $8 million Ranology Center. Dingleberry, who made his fortune late in life marketing Hula-Hoops, developed a fondness for Fauntleroy's frog collection while a student here. In later visits to the campus, he was distressed by the increasing dilapidation and poor maintenance of the collection. As a sixty-seven-year-old bachelor, he realized he would have no heirs and he offered the college his fortune. Upon the administration's enthusiastic acceptance of his gift, Dingleberry delivered an unusual stipulation in a stern speech made at the Board of Trustees' annual meeting: "In view of the fact that this fine college was founded in part to house Fauntleroy's frogs, the administration's negligence of the collection is a disgrace. For this reason, I am leaving my money to Mount Merry on the condition that it be used solely for the construction and maintenance of a center for frog studies. After all, Mount Merry owes everything to frogs!"

To this day, the school has honored his wishes in every detail and Dingleberry has never, on his frequent unannounced visits, been disappointed. Dingleberry's deep involvement with the $8 million Ranology Center extended to his personally choosing the faculty, recruited from universities across the world. Dingleberry himself reviews all applicants to the frog studies program and has power of veto over the independent admissions committee. Says Dingleberry, "We want to attract the higher caliber students who would not normally consider looking at Mount Merry."

Under the guidance of Prof. Newt Pickerel who holds the Fauntleroy Chair for Ranological Studies, the $8 million Mount Merry Ranology Center houses the most extensive Ranology program in the world. Every possible facet of frog studies is covered, ranging from the biological and ecological to the culinary and the decorative. The faculty is comprised of the brightest minds in Ranology who, according to Dingleberry's wishes, are more than adequately compensated for their endeavors. Both students and faculty enjoy the most modern of facilities in the fully air-conditioned and heated eighteen-story structure. Spectacular features inside include tank capacity for more than three thousand frogs, a complete indoor lily pond, insect breeding

HOW MEN WERE TURNED INTO FROGS

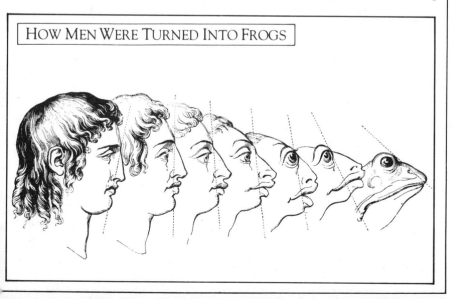

ground to provide snacks, and the voluminous frog morgue where refrigerated file drawers contain every specimen of every frog known to mankind. The $8 million Center is also distinguished by the landmark topiary garden honoring the numerous frog species and the Ranology faculty parking lot which is always filled with shiny Mercedes and Jaguars.

The course of study in the Ranology Department is completely separate from the rest of Mount Merry's program and Ranology students are advised not to mingle with Mount Merry's student body. To make sure that they won't, Dingleberry has graciously made his home available as a dormitory for Ranology majors to heighten their sense of camaraderie. A real *esprit de corps* is fostered by the rigorous course of study that all Ranology students must follow. As the program has been carefully planned, there are no electives.

A typical day in the life of the Ranology Center might be like this:

6:00 A.M.	Rise
6:30 A.M.	Breakfast
7:00 A.M.	Jog to $8 million Ranology Center
8:00 A.M.	Arrive at $8 million Ranology Center
8:15 A.M.	History of Frogs
11:15 A.M.	Insect Breeding for Frog Nutrition
1:15 P.M.	Lunch
1:30 P.M.	Frog Psychoanalysis
3:30 P.M.	Dissection: Autopsy and Taxidermy
5:30 P.M.	Jog back to Dingleberry's
6:30 P.M.	Arrive at Dingleberry's and Dine
7:00 P.M.	Supervised Study Period
9:30 P.M.	Free Time—Write Letters Home
9:45 P.M.	Prepare for Bed
10:00 P.M.	Frog as Trope in European Story-Telling Tradition
10:30 P.M.	Lights Out

Applicants interested in the Ranology Program should contact Reuben Dingleberry and demonstrate their sincere interest in frog studies.

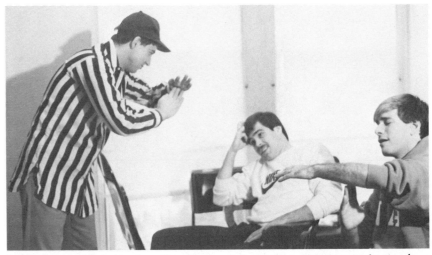

PHOTO BUG

In his Athletic Officiating class, Steve E. Dore helps students with those tricky signals.

INTERDISCIPLINARY ELECTIVES

The interdisciplinary electives are specific fields of study that, while not substantial enough to count as majors, nonetheless present a coherent and rewarding examination of topics that interest both students and faculty. Owing to their overwhelming popularity, students may not choose a course until sophomore year and then are limited to one per semester. It should be noted that interdisciplinary electives do not satisfy distribution requirements. Because some of them provide training in pre-vocational areas, many students find that of all the courses they took at Mount Merry these were the only useful ones in helping them find a job.

AMERICAN STUDIES

AS/$3:
THE AMERICAN MUSICAL
A star-studded salute to the showstopping moments of America's contribution to theater. Attention will be paid to the sets, the costumes, the choreography, Ethel Merman, and—oh, that music!

REV. BRUCE CADEMYTE

AS/1967–1:
NATIVE AMERICANS
A sober discussion of the tragic history of our native American peoples and their continual oppression by white imperialists who took away their land. Work includes listening to the records of Buffy Sainte-Marie and Cher.

GRETCHEN INDIGO

AS/1967–2:
CALIFORNIA'S COMING OF AGE AS A CULTURAL POWER IN AMERICAN SOCIETY
The advent of California as a state of mind: the Beach Boys, Disneyland, Wolfman Jack, Berkeley, Haight-Ashbury, Monterey Pop, Marin County, Venice Beach, est, Esalen, hot tubs, and Linda Ronstadt.

GRETCHEN INDIGO

AS/1776:
CORN
A study of the native American crop in all its permutations: Silver Queen, Country Gentleman, Butter and Sugar, hasty pudding, grits, Wayne Newton, Pollyanna, Bob Hope, Norman Rockwell, Lassie, Jell-O molds, and Minnie Pearl.

KINGSTON MILDEW

AS/12 oz.:
THE AMERICAN FAMILY
A survey of the concept of the nuclear unit since the 1950s. Role models include: the Ricardos, the Nelsons, the Cleavers, the Kramdens, the Flintstones, the Clampetts, the Bradys, the Partridges, the Bunkers, the Jeffersons, and the Ewings.

DOWNING BEERY

CHILD STUDIES

CHS/1967:
THE CHILD AND THE FAMILY
How to buy children's clothes, how to decorate a child's room, how to cook for children's palates. Including hand-me-downs, cribs, bunks, and bassinets, teaching nine-year-olds to eat liver, removing grass stains from sneakers.

GRETCHEN INDIGO, with CORDUROY

CHS/1066:
THE CHILD AND SOCIETY
An examination of the child's place in an adult world; the concept of being "seen but not heard," curtsying, bowing and kissing guests, table manners, standing up when adults enter a room, and sitting still for portraits.

LORD PENNYLACKING

CHS/33⅓:
TEACHING CHILDREN TO SING
Basic instruction in teaching children to sing before they can carry a tune, with emphasis on clapping in time with little dimpled hands, lisping and other adorable speech impediments such as pronouncing "R" as "W," gazing skyward while singing ballads.

LEROI PAXTON

CHS/B.C.:
TOTEMS OF CHILDHOOD

Starving children in India, the boogeyman, bedbugs who bite, the tooth fairy, Santa Claus, and the urgent necessity for a night light as nocturnal safeguard.

EARL E. MANN

CHS/4 to 6:
PROBLEMS OF CHILDHOOD

The concerns and challenges that plague children in their early years: eating paste and chalk, learning to tie shoes, riding a bicycle, saying the multiplication tables, writing script, and mastering the use of blunt scissors.

CASPAR Q. WIMPLEY

COSMETOLOGY

COS/1967:
NATURAL COSMETICS

Making good things for your face and body from the good things nature gives us. Masks (cucumber, yogurt, egg white, honey, and oatmeal), henna for hair and body, fruit-scented soaps and shampoos, stimulating hair growth by not washing it, and the uses of lemons as bleach and deodorant.

GRETCHEN INDIGO

COS/69:
DEPILATION

The complex and bristly question of removing unwanted body hair to enhance feminine allure. Issues examined include bleaching, shaving, waxing, chemical depilatories, and electrolysis, the final solution.

IRMA FEELEY

COS/$3–1:
MALE COSMETICS

The burgeoning field of men's cosmetics, from after-shave and cologne to facial treatments and bronzing gel. Shampoos, conditioners, hair spray and hair dryers, and the controversy about eye shadow and blushers.

REV. BRUCE CADEMYTE

COS/$3–2:
CAREERS IN HAIR MAINTENANCE

The demands, challenges, and rewards of dynamic careers in hair care: how to maintain an air of discretion (and when to drop it), plausible flattery, the choosing of shampoo robes, dressing rooms, music, and magazines, and sensing how much the market will bear in fees.

REV. BRUCE CADEMYTE

COS/100%:
THE ECONOMICS OF BEAUTY

A fiscally-oriented approach to the business of beauty, including the wisdom of using a French-sounding name, the cachet of a fashionable address, the crucial impact of packaging, and the overriding importance of an alluring spokeswoman.

HUGO MARKUP

JOURNALISM

JO/100G's:
WRITING HEADLINES

The skill of writing an attention-grabbing headline regardless of the content of the story and without recourse to pronouns. Attention will be paid to pathos, bathos, blood-and-guts, and such key words as "murder," "molest," "maniac," and "mother."

LAMBERT GLIBB

JO/100%:
THE HUMAN INTEREST STORY

How to find the human angle in any story: the jilted girlfriend, the motherless child, the cuckolded husband, the displaced elderly, homeless pets, and spunky orphans. Seeking out the milk of human kindness—and milking it dry.

HUGO MARKUP

JO/12 oz.:
REPORTING ON PEOPLE

The complex and exciting task of covering the activities of world leaders, politicos, media stars, celebrities, and hangers-on. Focus will center on building a network of reliable sources, checking facts when advisable, crashing parties, faking introductions, and making subjects identifiable while retaining their anonymity.

DOWNING BEERY

JO/1,000 V:
THE INTERVIEW

An examination of the techniques and ploys involved in extracting the information you want from the interview subject, including concealed recording devices, feigned sympathy, startlingly direct questions, making confessions that inspire further confidence, and other reassuring mannerisms.

NORMAN BATES

JO/#5:
WRITING REVIEWS

Building and using a reputation as a critic and a reviewer. The power to make or break a book or play; the opportunities to foster or finish careers, especially those of actresses who snubbed you once at a party. Discussions will include criteria by which to judge talent, good looks, declining reputations, and current voguishness. Attention will be paid to larding your reviews with sentences that cry out to be quoted in ads.

FRANK LLOYD KOVALCHICK

TRANSPORTATION

TRANS/8″:
CARS

The automobile as a mobile environment: the need for the right make for the guy on the go, tips on interior decoration, stereo systems, and customizing; also, the potential of the back seat for social interaction, how to deal with such obstacles as stick shifts and bucket seats. Includes tips on parallel parking.

BRUNO COXMAN

TRANS/00:
BUSES

An in-depth study of the most widespread mode of public transportation. Course features walking tour of all Waterbury bus routes and examination of every bus stop, as well as a study of bus design, including how kneeling buses do it. Prerequisite: exact change.

STEVE E. DORE

TRANS/1776:
TRAINS

A nostalgic retrospective of the great era of train travel. In thrilling lectures illustrated with his own black-and-white slides, Professor Mildew recalls the historic moments he has witnessed, beginning with the driving of the Golden Spike linking the Central Pacific and Union Pacific Railroads. With discussion of the lines that made America great, including the Atchison, Topeka, & Santa Fe, the Erie-Lackawanna, and the Chattanooga Choo-choo.

KINGSTON MILDEW

TRANS/π:
PLANES

What keeps them up in the air.

IRVING KLUPFERBERG

TRANS/III:
SHOES

Back to basics for cheap, safe, sensible transportation. A podiatric overview: the superiority of the oxford; polishing techniques and the wisdom of shoe trees; sneakers and the onset of moral decay; and the controversy about flip-flops—are they acceptable off the beach? Some attention will be paid to the dangers of high heels.

H.A.G. KLUMPP

PHOTO BUG

Winter term is a special time at Mount Merry.

WINTER TERM

WINTER TERM IS A special time at Mount Merry. Although classes are held as usual, the spirited selection of course offerings, reflecting the faculty's favorite topics, inspires an enthusiasm and vitality that everyone feels. Winter term provides the Mount Merry community with the opportunity to delve into particular interests and obsessions for which there is too little time during the regular academic year. Although it is an unstructured, unpressured time in which students are required to take only one course, many students can't resist taking a full load of courses. Because Winter term courses carry double credit, enthusiastic students find they can easily satisfy requirements for graduation in this relaxed, easy atmosphere. For the convenience of students wishing to fulfill required courses, condensed versions of the two required courses—History of Mount Merry taught by Dr. Kaiser and Elementary Frog Studies taught by Prof. Newt Pickerel—are offered and are annually filled to capacity. The Winter term program is enriched by non-credit courses also taught by the faculty which have included in recent years: breadmaking, juggling, ham radio operating, massaging, speed-reading, coloring, and driving a stick shift.

Classics	It's All Greek to Me—Cademyte
History	The Entire History of Mankind—Mildew
Legal Studies	Grand Larceny: Your Rights—McGillicuddy
Folklore	The Iconography of the Rainbow—Indigo
Economics	Inflation in Canada—Glibb
Biology	Sex: Does It Make a Difference?—Feeley
Sociology	Intellectual Frauds—Pennylacking
Anthropology	World Cultures: Palm Springs—Mann
Art	The Brushwork of Jackson Pollock—Kovalchick
Business	Fast Food Chains—Markup
Chemistry	The Chemistry of Wine-Making—Rush
Computer Science	Fun with Fractions—Klupferberg
Development Studies	How to Say Hello—The O'Kays
English	A Good Dictionary: Your Guide and Friend—Wimpley
Education	Recess—Mrs. Rogers
Foreign Languages	Speaking in Tongues—Le Pue
Geology	Strip Mining—Wether
Home Economics	Vacuuming Upholstery—Klumpp
Mass Communications	The Nielsen Family: a Profile—Beery
Mathematics	Zen and the Domains of Holomorphy—Gamble
Eastern Studies	Dealing with Another Culture—Wop
Music	The Genius of Rex Smith—Paxton
Philosophy	Looking Out for Number One—Coxman
Physical Education	Controlling Your Breath—Dore
Physics	Greta Garbo—Franklin
Politics	Gerald Ford—Goldman
Psychology	Understanding Elementary Phenomena—Bates
Religion	Footwear in the Bible—Savonarola
Speech	The Gettysburg Address—De Thugg

PHOTO BUG

Bruno Coxman expounds his playboy philosophy.

SAMPLE PROGRAMS

THE SAMPLE PROGRAMS below will give some idea of the usual process by which students arrive at the course schedule that best serves—and forms—their interests. These programs are merely suggested samples, but they reflect patterns of study seen again and again at Mount Merry. Asterisks designate required courses or courses taken to fulfill distribution requirements.

PRE-PHILOSOPHER
(Student placed out of English, Religion, and Art requirements.)

FALL	WINTER TERM	SPRING
Freshman year		
Chemistry in Action*	History of Mount Merry*	Recreational Chemistry
The Works of Carlos Castaneda	Chemistry of Wine-Making	Personality and Social Relations
Sophomore year		
Sensations	Looking Out for Number 1	Residual Effects of Alcohol on the Body
	Elementary Frog Studies*	
Junior Year		
Epicureanism	Gerald Ford	LOAF
	The Nielsen Family: a Profile	
Senior year		
Continental Philosophy	World Cultures: Palm Springs	Playboy Philosophy
	Sex: Does it Make a Difference?	
	Speaking in Tongues	

PRE-BUSINESS
(Student placed out of English, Religion, and Art requirements.)

FALL	WINTER TERM	SPRING
Freshman year		
History of Mount Merry*	World Cultures: Palm Springs	Quantitative Methods
Elementary Frog Studies*		Dollars and Cents
Historical Geology*		Dull Normal Mathematics
Introduction to Advertising*		Oral Communications
Sophomore year		
Personal Finance	Strip Mining	Investing in the Law
The Eastern Market		Anthropology of Tourism
Petroleum and Its Implications		Wealth and Poverty in Greece and Rome
Erotic Nature (dropped after 2 weeks)		Elementary Conversational French

PHOTO BUG

"Don't spill any!" explains H.A.G. Klumpp to an eager student of laundry.

Junior year
Foreign Study Tour: Money
  in Europe

Senior year

Tax-Free Gifts	Fast Food Chains	Law and the Resourceful
Creative Writing	Grand Larceny: Your Rights	Criminal
Advanced Persuasion		Geology Survey

PRE-DOMESTIC

FALL	WINTER TERM	SPRING

Freshman year

Ritual in Everyday Life	Genius of Rex Smith	Interior Engineering
American Folk Dancing		Food Chemistry
Domestic Management		Sociology of the Family
Laundry Problems		American Folk Dancing
		(repeat for credit)

Sophomore year

Gastronomical Geometry	How to Say Hello	Body Building and
Microwave Studies		Slenderizing
La Cuisine de France		Natural Cosmetics
Epicureanism		Depilation
		Body Language
		Body Image and the Aesthetic
		Experience

Junior year

Meat Appreciation (dropped after 2 lectures)	Sex: Does It Make a Difference?	Stress
Introduction to China		Human Potential
Gemstones as Investment		Personal Growth
Christian Marriage and Family*		Female Development
Language of Romance		

Senior year

Home Ec Practicum	Vaccuming Upholstery	Elementary Frog Studies*
Shoes		History of Mount Merry*
Market Policy		Xerography*
Remedial Television		American Decorative Arts*
		Our Bodies, Our Selves*

PHOTO BUG

Frisbee games are a familiar sight.

ALTERNATIVES TO EDUCATION

ROTC

THE ARMY ROTC PROGRAM was established to provide at college-level institutions like Mount Merry a program which will attract, ensnare, and sentence gullible students into serving in the U.S. Army. The underlying philosophy of the ROTC program is that the education of prospective military leaders must capture the caliber of the academic and social milieu that distinguishes our nation's voluntary armed forces today. Nowhere are these standards better met than here at Mount Merry. One great virtue of the ROTC program is that the student can major in practically any academic field because absolutely no course of study will have any bearing on army life.

All interested students should report to Col. Ulysses Hawk. Responsibilities include wearing a cadet uniform at all times and enrolling in Colonel Hawk's Adventures in Leadership courses which are designed to challenge the student and introduce him to such vital military subject areas as potato peeling, deck swabbing, and toilet cleaning. Students desirous of an ROTC scholarship may apply on a competitive basis to Colonel Hawk's Boot Camp Scholarship Contest. Students who survive the rigorous ordeal receive all tuition, fees, books, and permission to borrow Colonel Hawk's jeep for dates. Completion of a four-year military studies program would qualify the student for a commission as a second lieutenant in the regular United States Army or the United States Army Reserve. However, Mount Merry has no military studies program. Thus her ROTC graduates qualify as privates.

FOREIGN STUDY

The interesting influence of study abroad is generally recognized as healthy and enriching, and Mount Merry is eager to encourage her students to spend a semester or several at educational institutions abroad, or, for that matter, anywhere outside Waterbury. (It should be noted, of course, that students pay full tuition and dormitory fees to Mount Merry for the semesters of their absence, as well as any fees accruing to the host institution, or additional costs such as air fare, postage, or bail.)

Though foreign study is clearly pertinent to such courses of study as foreign languages, history, and art history, it is neither advisable nor profitable in other fields of specialization, such as geology or physical education. Therefore, students whose principal aim at Mount Merry is spending junior year in the cafés and boulevards of Europe are advised to plan their programs well in advance with Professor Le Pue, counselor for study abroad. Students who leave for Europe without previously notifying him (a post card from the airport is *insufficient notice*) are regarded as having withdrawn from the college, and must pay severe penalties to have themselves reinstated as students.

Aside from its program in Liverpool, Mount Merry has no foreign study opportunities of its own, so students wishing to study somewhere else are urged to apply directly to the foreign university, foreign study group, or any accredited institution. Mount Merry will accept full credit toward graduation from any institution of learning whose accreditation seems remotely legitimate.

Students are required, upon return to campus, to account for their time abroad. They may choose to keep a diary of their European experiences (the First Amendment is strictly observed), to write weekly letters to Professor Le Pue, or to work up a project which demonstrates a skill they may have learned during their absence. Wine tastings, map reading sessions, and lectures on the Italian postal system are among the possibilities.

AWARDS

1. **The Hildegarde Klumpp Award for Faith,** awarded annually to the female student who, in the judgment of the college chaplain, has demonstrated persistent faith in matters beyond her understanding.

2. **The Agnes Klumpp Award for Hope,** awarded annually to the female student who, in the judgment of the college chaplain, has demonstrated persistent hope in situations beyond her control.

3. **The Gertrude Klumpp Award for Charity,** awarded annually to the female student who, in the judgment of the college chaplain, has demonstrated persistent charity in matters beyond her financial means.

4. **The Patrick Donahue McSorley Award,** established in memory of Bishop McSorley by his loving brothers. The income on this fund, derived from the family brewery, provides each annual winner with a connoisseur's tour through Europe, including the vineyards of France, the beer gardens of Germany, and the stills on the Isle of Skye. The winner is selected by Prof. Downing Beery on the basis of the most imaginative application to the task of drinking liquor. Thanks to the award's source of income, this is the most remunerative prize offered at Mount Merry.

5. **The Fauntleroy Prize,** established by Reuben Dingleberry in 1961 to commemorate the beloved inspiration of the school, annually honors the Ranology student who, in the opinion of Mr. Dingleberry, most deeply empathizes with frogs and shows greatest loyalty to the spirit of Fauntleroy.

6. **The Garland Rooney Prize** is awarded annually to the student who best demonstrates excellence as a human being.

7. **The Brenda Diana Duff Frazier Prize** is awarded annually to the student who, in the eyes of the selection committee headed by Lord Pennylacking, exemplifies the neatness, politeness, and punctuality that give dignity and a sense of purpose to Caucasian youth across the nation.

8. **The Mildred Maim Virtue Is Its Own Reward Award** was established in 1975 by the alumni of the Carrie Nation Temperance College in honor of the departing headmistress and is awarded to the female student who, in the opinion of Prof. Bruno Coxman, unyieldingly demonstrates the dignity of chastity throughout her years at Mount Merry by always saying "no." Due to Professor Coxman's rigorous screening process, the prize is not always awarded annually.

9. **The Classics Award** is given annually to the male senior who, in the opinion of Rev. Bruce Cademyte, possesses the most classic set of features of all the men at Mount Merry. The award provides for studying and cruising the Aegean with Reverend Cademyte during the summer following the award.

10. **The Mildred Maim Scholarship Award** was established in 1954 by the then headmistress directly upon her arrival at the Carrie Nation Temperance College to honor the junior with the highest academic average. In 1975, upon Carrie Nation's merger with Mount Merry, a second Mildred Maim Scholarship Award was established to similarly recognize the male junior with

PHOTO BUG

The Mildred Maim Scholars proudly sport their badges of merit.

the highest average. The award consists of a scroll, a sash, and a tiara for each winner. Tradition dictates that Mildred Maim Scholars wear their awards at all times during their senior year (including off-campus visits). It should be noted that winners will be held financially responsible for loss or damage to these awards which are handed down to succeeding years' recipients.

11. **The Spirit of Mount Merry Award** is a citation conferred on the Mount Merry student who best embodies the unique qualities of the school. The medal bearing the school seal is awarded annually to the student who demonstrates stoicism in the face of academic limitation, pragmatism in the setting of personal goals, modesty in scholastic achievement, and remarkable initiative in social intercourse.

12. **The Very Reverend Lamont Dozier Carver Award** is presented annually by the chaplain to the student who has proven himself to be a credit to the school by virtue of his ceaseless cooperation and selfless devotion to the chaplain. In keeping with the spirit of humility and sacrifice thus honored, this award carries with it no remunerative or material reward.

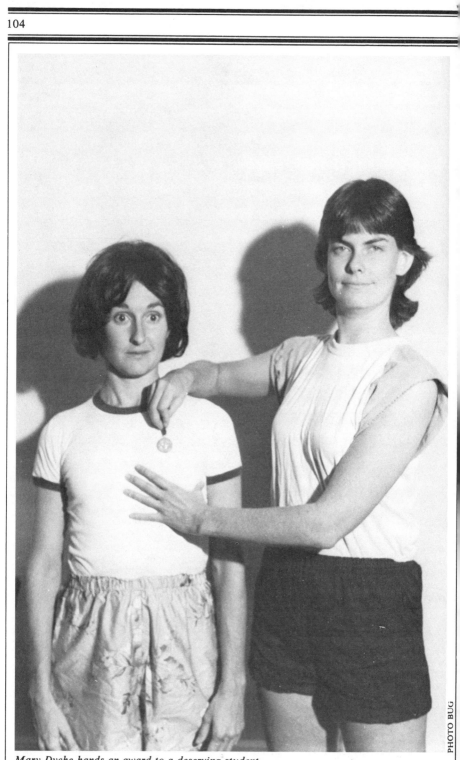

PHOTO BUG

Mary Dyche hands an award to a deserving student.

13. **The Christian Fellowship Award** is bestowed yearly to that member of Undergraduates for God in the Humanities (UGH) who has done the most to spread the Gospel in concrete terms. This prize is given for the student's gift in witnessing, which is measured in quantitative terms via body count.

14. **The Saskatchewan Society of Certified Public Accountants Annual Award** of a vintage manual adding machine to two senior accounting majors who have evidenced an interest in public accounting, and who have maintained high class averages.

15. **The Fishwick-Buchanan Essay Prize,** a plastic change purse containing approximately $23, the income derived from a gift of the late Howard Fishwick, Sr. ('46), provides an annual award to the leading essay submitted by student or faculty member on the life or works of James Buchanan.

16. **The Hugo Markup Profit and Loss Award** conferred annually by Prof. Hugo Markup to the business major with the strongest balance sheet at the end of the year. The prize consists of a certificate for twenty shares of Penn Central stock.

17. **The Creative Writing Award** was established to emphasize the importance of creative writing in everyday life. The prize awards $100 plus duplicating costs to the student who submits the most convincing resumé in the eyes of Prof. Lambert Glibb. The award carries with it Mount Merry's verification of all claims made in the resumé.

18. **The Crepes Suzette Award** is given annually to the female student who best satisfies Prof. Pepe Le Pue in mastering the fine art of French.

19. **The Hazel Nutt Psychological Stress Award** was established in memory of her late son, P. Nutt (1942–1960) to honor the student who has offered the most selfless assistance to Prof. Norman Bates in his ongoing exploration of new dimensions in psychology. The award shall be given to the family in the event that student is no longer capable of accepting it for himself.

20. **The Captain Flint Elocution Award** is granted to the winner of Leon De Thugg's annual Speech Bee in which points are accumulated for the correct pronunciation of difficult words, such as "multisyllabic," and "dictionary."

21. **The Kingston Mildew History Award** is presented to the history major in the graduating class.

22. **The Demetra Papyannou Photography Prize** is presented by Spiridion Papyannou in honor of his mother. The award is given to the student who has made outstanding achievements in the field of photography in the opinion of Mr. Papyannou who develops all student snapshots at Spiro's Camera Nook in Waterbury. The prize consists of a cartridge of Kodak C126-12 film.

23. **The Northwestern Connecticut Chapter of the Tapioca Manufacturers Association Home Economics Prize** is awarded at the Tapioca Manufacturers annual cook-off to the student who plans and cooks the tastiest five-course meal in which each dish contains a significant amount of tapioca. The winner receives a ten percent discount on all further purchases of tapioca.

24. **The Timothy Leary Chemistry Award** is conferred by Prof. Rob Rush on the first-year student who evidences the most promise in the application of creative chemistry. The award consists of five grams.

25. **The Florence Ballard Music Award** honors the senior who clearly demonstrates outstanding vocal ability in singing word particles, adaptability, and a willingness to work with others. The prize carries with it a one-year studio contract to sing backup for Mr. LeRoi Paxton.

26. **The Daily Frog Journalism Prize** for a senior whose regular contributions to the student newspaper exemplify the principles of popular and colorful journalism. The winner receives a one-year subscription to the *New York Post*.

SERVICING THE STUDENTS

CAREER COUNSELING

MOUNT MERRY TAKES very seriously her obligations to her students, believing firmly that they extend beyond the mere four (or more) years of academic experience. The Career Counseling Center recognizes the need to integrate the abstract ideals of the school's liberal arts education with professional and career preparation.

The primary goal of the center is to provide direction to students who are confused about their "talents" and how they can best be employed in the job market. (Students who plan careers in professional fields such as medicine, law, or finance are advised to consult with family members or other contacts in similar fields, and with the Educational Testing Service.)

Facilities at the counseling center include an extensive library of career materials comprised of at least one hundred pamphlets filed in alphabetical order in the bottom drawer of the Career Counseling Filing Cabinet. Also on file are sample resumés which have garnered jobs for students in the past. Presiding over this collection is Arnold Botcher, whose extensive job credits include experiences as dishwasher, encyclopedia salesman, postman, lifeguard, gas station attendant, bellhop, stock boy, baby sitter, and messenger.

Botcher spends many hours listening to students' career concerns and offering words of encouragement. He is also responsible for bringing to the campus representatives from popular professions who speak to the students about the rewards of their particular fields.

HEALTH SERVICES

The Les Malingering Health Center is a wing of the Aurelia Slouch E-Z Rest Funeral Home in downtown Waterbury, easily reached from campus by public transportation. Ably administered by Nurse Aurelia Slouch (who provides a two-for-one discount when her mortuary skills are required), the Health Center is further staffed by volunteers from the Biology Department as well as curious Ranology students.

Each student is required to enter a group accident medical insurance policy directly contracted with Nurse Aurelia Slouch. Under the terms of this contract, Nurse Slouch pledges to arrive at the scene of an accident in an amount of time deemed reasonable by her. Students are strongly discouraged from seeking private health care, even in emergencies. This contract provides for office visits, preliminary diagnosis, and up to forty-five-minute confinements in the three-bed and two-sleeping bag infirmary wing.

Individual and confidential appointments for the discussion of birth control, venereal disease, and sexual technique may be made with freelance gynecological consultant Prof. Bruno Coxman. Students requiring contraception may order directly from the Campus Family Planning Warehouse.

COUNSELING SERVICE

One of the most frequently used facilities on the Mount Merry campus is the Psychological Studies Center. The PsychoCenter offers a range of counseling services including advisory sessions with sophomores who plan to major in psychology. Students with more urgent needs are advised to call the Suicide Hotline for counseling and information on method, efficiency, and pain-quotient. The number to call is 555-7596 (not to be confused with 555-7597 which is the number of Joe's Pizza Parlor). In addition, students who want professional attention may make appointments with Dr. Alexander Lucre (financing available from Waterbury Savings at eighteen percent).

PET CLINIC

The Pet Clinic is located at the service entrance to the Lucrezia Borgia Dining Hall where veterinarian Dinah N. Kitchen provides out-patient services including diagnosis, minor surgery, and all vaccinations for students' pets. For details, *go in person* to her office after breakfast on weekdays. In case of a deceased pet, bereaved students must grant Dr. Kitchen full jurisdiction over the disposal of the animal's remains.

PHOTO BUG

Representatives from various professions often come to recruit on campus.

PHOTO BUG

Students absorbed in the joy of learning are a common sight on Mount Merry's campus.

WHAT WILL MY LIFE BE LIKE?

WHILE ACADEMICS IS A major part of the Mount Merry experience, there *is* life outside the classroom (and we don't mean the biology lab!!!). Our policy of mandatory campus residence insures that all our students will work together in finding ways to live with each other. Although Mount Merry is a small community, students learn that size doesn't matter—a lesson that is applicable all through life. Student life is as diverse as the students who live it. The friends you will meet here may be casual or intimate, the dormitories may inspire camaraderie or complaints, the activities may be interesting or educational, and the "special people," well, those are the ones you really get to know and at Mount Merry there's a lot more of them than you'd ever expect. Yet despite this diversity, the common interests of the students who have chosen or ended up at this school bind them all together and for many this means friendships that will last for four years, if not a lifetime.

There are other members of our community who will affect your life at Mount Merry. Every faculty member is a potential neighbor, and you are likely to see your anatomy teacher at lunch, a basketball game, at the Padded Cell, or in a late-night bull session in your dorm. You may even find yourself, after the first reel of a campus film showing or in between halves of the game or while making the bed, discussing with him the merits of the entertainment. In this way, you can get to know your professors better, which improves your academic awareness and your grade point average.

With so many people putting in such an input into the community, there is an energy on the Mount Merry campus. You can sense it. Smell it. Even students sitting quietly under a tree generate an aroma of high intellectual pursuit. From the happy odors of meals in the dining halls, to the smell of perspiration pouring off students involved in our many athletic endeavors, to the breath of our older professors sharing insights with students as they amble across campus, Mount Merry is a bouquet of academic fragrances.

The college has tried to build a residential campus of beauty, variety, and utility, designed to accommodate the people who live there. It has been carefully laid out to assure quiet spaces for students who may want to have a relaxing conversation with friends and classmates. Although the campus is a world unto itself, you won't be isolated from the real world—downtown Waterbury is just a step away and you can buy a copy of the *New York Times* every morning from the Business Department's newsstand. Mount Merry students take advantage of Waterbury and its citizens almost daily—there is a post office, a dry cleaner, and a small but excellent movie theater that shows the finest in family entertainment as well as "businessmen's" matinees. In addition to providing these recreational facilities, Waterbury offers needy people to whom concerned students can deliver community service. For example, some students spend Thursday morning teaching a group of special students how to make Kleenex tissue carnations. Others travel to nursing homes or hospitals to host parties or bowling tournaments.

Even if you never leave the confines of the campus, there's plenty to distract you from your studies. Many academic interests bring students together—concerts, seminars, poetry readings, and political demonstrations. More often, it's the many parties, mixers, homecomings, Classics Department bacchanalia, and fancy dress affairs that give ample opportunities to form lasting friendships or nocturnal companionship. Mount Merry strives to develop students as whole people, which means that all aspects of life here relate to each other. You may study Shakespeare in English class, but your insights into his genius with character may be inspired by life on campus.

You may understand Falstaff more thoroughly from fêting on Greek row, or Caliban by living with your roommate, or Iago from a member of your study group. The Student Council for Affairs makes sure there's a lot of carrying on, including the weekly TGIF party where some students drink Coke or 7-Up and some drink beer.

Somewhere among the more than fifty officially recognized student organizations there is bound to be at least one to attract your interest. If not, you're free to start your own special interest group after consulting with the Psychological Studies Center. Of course, you don't have to be part of an organized activity to relax between studies, but Mount Merry doesn't encourage introversion. Involvement with issues and people is a cornerstone of self-growth. Such a homily is one of the many issues discussed each week in the "Food for Thought" seminars. At these, students and faculty gather in the Lucrezia Borgia Dining Hall to discuss some of the harder problems facing our generation in general and the campus in particular, from the assumptions underlying the American defense policy to the prevailing mood of "me-first" in our culture and its manifestations in some people on our campus. These seminars are well attended, not just because they're compulsory, but because of the lively debates and the delicious Twinkies and Kool-Aid refreshments.

Downing Beery poses for his picture.

PHOTO BUG

TRADITIONAL COLLEGE ACTIVITIES

Candlelight Ceremony

In the early fall, the senior class conducts the Candlelight Ceremony to induct the freshman class into the fraternity of Mount Merry students. Traditionally held on the lawn one warm September evening, the seniors pass lighted candles and other joint offerings—symbolizing the light of knowledge and commitment to higher education—to their freshmen brethren.

Homecoming Weekend

Parents, family, friends, and paramours are all invited to join us in the most exciting sporting event of the year—the match between the crew and football teams. After the body count, there is a gala reception at Prof. Downing Beery's house. Many middle-aged celebrants from Waterbury and its surrounds have been known to apply for midterm admission the following day.

Sophomore Buddy Night

Every Halloween, at a festive costume party, each freshman discovers the identity of his or her mysterious sophomore "buddy" who has been treating him or her with surprise presents and candy during the preceding week. Upon his or her unveiling, the sophomore then presents the freshman with the bill for all the week's gifts.

Sybarite Festival

A break in the grind of Fall term exams, the Sybarite Festival allows students to escape to the ancient Greek city of Sybaris, thanks to Rev. Bruce Cademyte's convincing decorations and catering in the Lucrezia Borgia Dining Hall. Commencing with a "Feast of Virgins" and culminating in a chariot race starring Flicka and Misty, the festival is characterized by continuous libations of grain punch. Students customarily enjoy the festivities right up until their next exam the following day.

Mardi Gras/Ash Wednesday

Students and faculty alike celebrate Shrove Tuesday by wearing funny costumes from the Art Department to all their classes. At day's end they join in a parade around campus, showered with confetti supplied by the Computer Studies Department. The highlight of this soiree is the dunking of the highly reluctant Reverend Savonarola in Fauntleroy Pond. Confession begins promptly at 6:00 A.M. the following Wednesday and all dining facilities are closed for the next forty days.

Parents' Weekend

Parents, relatives, and friends have an opportunity to become acquainted with Mount Merry life as it really is because Parents' Weekend is held in the middle of the week when students are in classes and studying. Parents are invited to attend classes, eat in the dining halls, participate in the athletic program, and sleep in the dorms.

Fauntleroy Day

Beginning with a memorial service in Brother Torquemada Chapel that lasts the entire morning, the Mount Merry community takes a day off to salute the spiritual inspiration of the school—Fauntleroy. Reuben Dingleberry conducts a compulsory tour through the Fauntleroy Museum in Fauntleroy House and then allows interested non-Ranology students a once-a-year chance to see the interior of the $8 million Ranology Center (Ranology students serve as monitors protecting the $8 million Center from the too-curious). That evening, the Ranology students host a formal dance on the $8 million Ranology Center Plaza, that the rest of Mount Merry is free to observe.

College Picnic

The end of classes in the spring is marked by a college-wide picnic on campus at which the Home Economics Department offers their best culinary efforts over the past year. Frisbee, volleyball, kite-flying, and other spontaneous activities characterize this event.

Students queuing up for the Foreign House bathroom.

The fun-filled atmosphere of communal living.

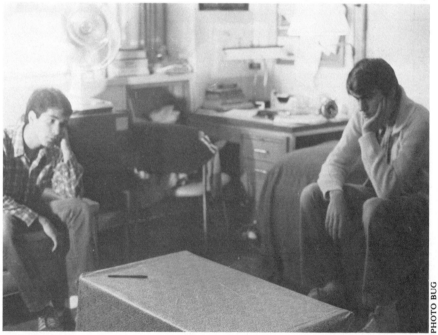

PHOTO BUG

PHOTO BUG

WHERE WILL I SLEEP?

The informal and accidental interchange between students' varied backgrounds, cultures, and intellectual activities is enriched and expanded by Mount Merry's various housing arrangements. The administration believes that students' natural attraction to each other will bring them together and result in interesting combinations and experiences that will enlarge the Mount Merry experience. Therefore students are required to live on campus, unless they have previously arranged to live with a married blood relative (brother, sister, parent, or grandparent) who lives in a twenty-mile radius.

Dorm life at Mount Merry is relatively structured. It is monitored by resident advisers appointed by the Holy Office; they can be seen patrolling the halls, indentifiable by their red badges and staffs of office. Some students find their presence comforting. As well as answering students' questions, they maintain discipline, overseeing obedience to such regulations as parietals (which allow greater concentration on sleep) and the pet rulings (no pets larger than a breadbox are allowed, and scaly pets discouraged).

The one exception to the rule is the Foreign House, where students sign up to live according to foreign traditions. They enjoy such exotic variations as lumpy double beds and scratchy brown toilet paper. Customs vary depending on the country in power. In recent months, the Foreign House has been surrounded by cows since the pro-Indira Indian faction took over. The scent of curry pervades the hallways and female residents of the Foreign House are recognizable on campus by their colorful saris. Depending on the flavor of the Foreign House, the waiting list varies from one week to four years. There are currently a number of openings.

The basic dorm accommodations for students are very comfortable; each student is guaranteed a bed, a desk, a chair, and the statutory minimum of square footage recommended by the Federal Housing Authority. (Students are advised to bring

More of the fun-filled atmosphere of communal living.

PHOTO BUG

PHOTO BUG

Mobile Units—picket fence extra (see School Comptroller Izzy A. Shyster).

sheets, curtains, a lamp, a wastebasket, and an alarm clock.) Most rooms on campus are doubles or triples, which increases togetherness between students and fosters an air of cooperation. A few dormitory facilities (notably the Mobile Units for Upper-class Males) are intended for one student only; students must demonstrate just cause or an inability to function within the community in order to qualify for this housing. Otherwise, rooms are assigned by a system of petition, lottery, or fiscal contribution.

Freshmen are traditionally housed together, a practice that unites the class and helps form friendships and other relationships very quickly. The freshmen men are allotted rooms in Project IV, a dormitory built by the WPA and famous on campus and elsewhere for its stark modern aesthetic. It stands on a hillside overlooking the women's dorm, with a path between them. The freshmen women are housed in the Emma Goldman Annex, Mount Merry's most modern building and masterpiece of minimalist architecture. Its solid glass walls provide plenty of light and exposure, and the ban on curtains assures that its showcase character will be maintained. (The minimalist motif is carried out even in the room furnishings which feature such innovations as bare concrete walls and handle-less doors.)

Sophomores at Mount Merry and upper-class students with no pull whatsoever live in Paternoster Hall, which was originally built as a monks' cloister. Constructed around a quad, it has separate entrances for men and women and there are no communicating passages between the sexes' rooms. Rooms in Paternoster are famous for their cozy, intimate atmosphere and antique air; standard furnishings include, as well as the usual bed and desk, a prie-dieu and devotional picture for each student.

Upper-class housing alternatives at Mount Merry are exciting; fraternity row allows members of the two fraternities and two sororities to live among students of their own type, a self-affirming experience. At Mount Merry the frat houses are former residential structures converted when they fell into the hands of the school. Finally completed is the Izzy A. Shyster Dormitory for Upper-Class Women (inhabited since 1978), built by the generosity of a Waterbury contractor with "surplus" materials from a famous motel chain. Special features include Mediterranean decor, twin double beds for each room, and a color TV for each co-ed. Many of the upper-class men do manage to qualify for the Mobile Unit Housing, consisting of self-contained units for each person. They are often grouped according to "themes"; recent years have seen such "Theme Parks" as sports, Waterbury Women, and beer. Though residents of the Mobile Units usually sign up for dining contracts, the kitchenettes with full-size refrigerators allow them a considerable advantage in entertainment possibilities. The resident advisers for the Theme Parks are chosen on the basis of size and combative skill, and are issued a German shepherd and a nightstick as well as the traditional badge of office.

Dorm rooms provide ample space for study or self-examination.

PHOTO BUG

Students anticipate another one of those potluck suppers.

PHOTO BUG

WHAT WILL I EAT?

One of Mount Merry's many great strengths is her wide variety of dining options to suit any preference. The unique system of punching a time clock to fulfill the dining requirement (students find the time clocks handily at the entrance to all dining facilities) avoids all kinds of administrative confusion. The strict system of hours for meal service adds an element of planning to otherwise unstructured student schedules, a feature some students come to depend upon.

The Lucrezia Borgia Dining Hall serves a variety of hot and cold entrees for a well-balanced diet. Special arrangements may be made for students on low-calorie, low-carbohydrate, vegetarian, low-sodium, Scarsdale, and Never-Say-Diet diets. The work-study program carried out with the cooperation of the Home Economics and Chemistry Departments allows a fresh element of unpredictability that keeps mealtimes from being boring. "Gourmet" meals are planned monthly, featuring foreign food and decorations, such as Mexican, Polynesian, and Antarctic.

There is also a health food dining hall, known affectionately by the students as "the root cellar." Its menu features such items as sprouts, granola, yogurt, honey, and vegetarian casseroles, which the students may mix at will. Occasional entertainment might include songs from the madrigal quartet or the campus mime troupe.

Some students like to change their routine from time to time by purchasing food at the Kampus Korner Kanteen (a time clock prominently displayed allows students to use purchases of packaged food to satisfy the dining requirement, as well as their appetites!). The KKK stocks such popular and nutritional snack foods as Hostess cupcakes, Kraft cheese facsimiles, refrigerated colas, and the complete line of Frito-Lay products.

Students who live in the Foreign House take their meals in the Foreign Dining Hall, but they may, by special written permission two weeks in advance, invite guests to share their meals there. Of course, the student must speak in a foreign language; at meal times the dining room of the Foreign House is a real United Nations and the odors of the exotic cuisines and the strange implements (like chopsticks!) lend an international air to the campus.

Institutional dining isn't the only option for students at Mount Merry. Though all students are urged under threat of disciplinary action to purchase twenty-one-meal weekly food contracts, other possibilities do occur. The School Comptroller Izzy A. Shyster Grocery Store makes available to students a wider variety of food items than the Kampus Korner Kanteen, at specially low prices for less-than-first quality items. The Home Economics Department runs an outlet store selling the results of students' stove-side attempts (customers must sign releases on purchase). Rumor has it that meals are served occasionally at the two fraternity and two sorority houses. And although cooking in the dormitory rooms is strictly forbidden, potluck suppers in the dormitories bring students together over an informal selection of covered dishes. Friendly faculty members often open their homes to students and exchange ideas over a pleasant meal or while students are doing the dishes afterwards.

Sample Menu

Soup:	Vegetarian Beef
Entree:	Boiled Hot Dogs
	Steamed Rolls
Vegetables:	Buttered Lima Beans
	Whipped Potatoes
	Baked Beans *or* Sauerkraut
Salad:	Iceberg Lettuce with Tomato Wedge and "French" Dressing
Dessert:	Chocolate Pudding with White Whipped Topping
Beverages:	Fruit-Flavored Drink
	Milk
	Water

WHAT ARE THE BUILDINGS LIKE?

Among the other qualities Mount Merry shares with those other great urban New England colleges—Harvard, Yale, and Columbia—is the felicitous integration of a pastoral academic environment with a bustling metropolitan atmosphere. Mount Merry has been especially fortunate in the harmonious blend of classic and innovative styles of architecture that have appeared on her campus as she has grown through the years. The compact nature of the setting has challenged all of Mount Merry's architects and has resulted in a series of buildings laid out in an intricate and interesting fashion.

THE STUDENT UNION CENTER —Erected in 1966 on the site of the former Connecticut Colony House (which collapsed during WONK's Tribute to the Beach Boys Hop), the Student Union Center displays all the hallmarks of the institutional architecture of the 1960s. Designed by an architect noted for his pioneering work in airports, SUC serves as the living room of the college and is the center of college community life where students go to relax and participate in out-of-class activities that foster well-rounded growth. SUC provides space for entertainment, recreation, extracurricular activities, and truancy. The four-story structure contains:

HAIR CARE CENTER—for unisex styling and cosmetology experiments
GARAGE—specializes in foreign transmissions and low-riders
BALLROOMS
MEDITATION CENTER—featuring mats and realistic wall mural depicting Sunset Over the
    Pacific
CASINO—closed to students under 21
CHECK CASHING
THE PADDED CELL—the student "hangout"
LOST AND FOUND—managed by School Comptroller Izzy A. Shyster
DARKROOMS—for budding photographers
VISITORS CENTER AND WAITING AREA
BUS DEPOT
STUDENT STORE—carries stationery, books, sundries and rations, college pennants, gym
    shorts, sweatshirts, engagement rings, tents, lawn mowers, small pets, landfill, Q-Tip
    swabs, and other student supplies
OUTDOOR RENTAL AREA

THE FERNQUIST MATH CENTER —Referred to by students as "the marble minus sign," the Math Center is a rectangular, three-story structure noted for its avant-garde design—white marble walls with absolutely no windows. Inside are classrooms, the vast computer lab, the electronic games room with its chess boards and pinball machines, and the spacious lobby where business majors set up tneir refreshment stands.

THE $8 MILLION RANOLOGY CENTER —The pride of the Mount Merry campus, the $8 million Ranology Center is an imposing eighteen-story building marking the latest in space-age design, circa 1961. Its architectonic grace is complemented by the beautiful eighteen-story bronze frog statue that adorns the front facade.

DOLITTLE HALL —The main academic building provides classrooms for the liberal arts courses that don't require labs. Features in this eighty-year-old neo-Gothic edifice include the original blackboards, desks, and gaslights kept in mint condition due to the students' respectful and infrequent use.

FAUNTLEROY HOUSE —The school's administrative building directly in front of Fauntleroy Pond. The handsome colonial structure houses Dr. Kaiser's and Dr. Fitzcox's offices, the bursar's, registrar's, and transcript office, and, in the Bauhaus-style new wing, School Comptroller Izzy A. Shyster's office and indoor tennis court.

PHOTO BUG

Emulating Demosthenes, students fill their mouths with pebbles and speak over the waves of Fauntleroy Pond.

BROTHER TORQUEMADA CHAPEL —The oldest structure at Mount Merry, and the most versatile. In addition to providing the college with a chapel for religious services, BTC functions also as a residence for Reverend Savonarola, who lives in the basement, and Rev. Bruce Cademyte, who dwells in the redecorated Lady Chapel. The Holy Office maintains their offices and workroom in the underlying catacombs. When not in use for religious purposes, the confessional booths do double duty as the language lab, as long as students remember to turn the switch to channel B, not C.

THE LUCREZIA BORGIA DINING ROOM —The college's premier dining facility is decorated in a lavish Gothic style that transports students to the days of fine manor living. The ornate architecture and clean tables offer a rarefied atmosphere for dining. Often the dining room is decorated for "theme nights," e.g., students may find themselves dining under a cardboard Mount Vesuvius on "Pompeii Night." Kitchen facilities are at the rear of the building.

THE HENRY MILLER LIBRARY —The college library is a sturdy brick building holding 18,000 books at last count. The library is carpeted for absorbing sound and the soft, luxurious leather reading chairs guarantee that students will spend many hours of uninterrupted peace studying and reflecting. With its vending machines and ashtrays, the lobby is often the scene of informal student get-togethers, while the open stacks afford opportunities both academic and social for students, outside visitors, and the like.

THE CHARO AUDITORIUM —The latest addition to the Mount Merry campus is the spacious auditorium for theater and other performance events. This modern amphitheater boasts several modern design concepts such as Vegas-style couch seats, a rising orchestra pit, an Al Jolson runway, and friendly full-bar waitress service.

THE ARTHUR VanDUUM BELL GYMNASIUM —The gymnasium provides facilities for basketball, squash, bowling, football, a natatorium for swimming, lockers, sauna, barbecue, wrestling cage, reducing rollers, Universal, Nautilus, and Polaris machines, and an "office" for Steve E. Dore. VanDuum Bell Gym currently houses all on-campus physical education activities, both academic and required extracurricular, and will do so until a substantial gift permits construction of adequate facilities.

PHOTO BUG

Father Savonarola points the way to Hell.

EXTRACURRICULAR ACTIVITIES

SPECIAL INTEREST GROUPS

THE DAILY FROG

Mount Merry's official newspaper is entitled the *Daily Frog*. Put out entirely by students (with the ever-present, enthusiastic assistance of adviser Prof. Procter Gamble), the *Daily Frog* appears every Friday. Dedicated students undertake all phases of producing a newspaper, from selling ads (sometimes resorting to the expert tutelage of School Comptroller Izzy A. Shyster) to setting type on a vintage Linotype machine purchased from the *Hartford Courant* in 1946.

As the official voice of the college, the *Frog* devotes a large portion of its space to college announcements of such essentials as the hours for confession and daily menus in the dining halls. The reporting staff has gained wide fame on campus for uncovering such riveting issues as the chalk-stealing ring that plagued the Math Department, and the source of H.A.G. Klumpp's extraordinary wardrobe.

EXPRESSIONS

Students who think they have talent for writing poetry or prose are encouraged to submit their efforts to the campus literary magazine, *Expressions*. Faculty adviser Steve E. Dore publishes any and all student poetry, stories, photography, and art work submitted. As a result, students are inspired to try anything and most of them do. Since Mr. Dore is unfamiliar with the concept of rewriting, many students prefer to concentrate on quantity rather than quality. Similar in format to the Waterbury phone book, *Expressions* is issued three times a year and, also like the phone book, is delivered free and unexpectedly at students' doors. The most prolific contributor is distinguished at term's end in a touching ceremony in which he lights the traditional bonfire composed of that year's issues of *Expressions*.

THE DIFFERENT DRUMMER

The *Different Drummer* is Mount Merry's alternative newspaper. Founded in 1972 to respond to a widely-perceived need (on the part of the students), the *Drummer* takes as its purpose the representation of students' concerns that may go uncovered by the *Daily Frog*. Resolved to accept no funding from the college in order to maintain complete freedom of expression, the *Drummer* depends on newsstand sales and charitable contributions (tax deductible: mail to Box 306, Mount Merry College; stamps accepted) to survive. Chronically understaffed and forced to make do with inadequate production facilities, the *Drummer* puts out an issue whenever it can; since its appearances are fewer than those of the *Frog* (which is rushed through production to serve as the major organ for the college) the *Drummer* is able to concentrate on more thoughtfully researched journalism and "think pieces." A notable issue last spring contained a hard-hitting critique of Kingston Mildew's teaching methods and an expose of alleged misuse of funds in Mount Merry's showcase $8 million Ranology Center.

PHOTO BUG

Mount Merry's compact campus located in the center of downtown Waterbury offers hundreds of opportunities for enthusiastic camera bugs, and the two darkrooms located in the cellar of the Student Union Center (SUC) offer further chances for students to refine their skills. The *Photo Bug*, published quarterly, compiles the best of these photographs in a magazine format. (Issues of the *Photo Bug* for the past two years are always on hand at the campus newsstand.)

Every spring, an outdoor photo show is held in the Kovalchick Memorial Shrubbery, an outdoor setting which shows the works to great advantage, particularly during the day. Frank Lloyd Kovalchick, the *Photo Bug* adviser, judges the show, awarding prizes for Best Picture, Best Lighting, Best Pose, Best Dog Portrait (canine), Best Dog Portrait (human), and so on.

The photographs illustrating the yearbook and this catalog are drawn from the *Photo Bug*'s archives, in the theory that Mount Merry's students can best do her justice.

MUSIC

Mount Merry provides many opportunities for vocal or other musical experience. The Religion Department Choir, which performs at all chapel services, is open to any students willing to attend the 6 A.M. rehearsals (membership in the choir does carry academic credit), and gives students who will sing at all the opportunity to become acquainted with a limited repertoire of sacred music. Two informal student-directed singing groups, The Mount Merry Melodies (all female) and the Pip Squeaks (all male) present programs of popular songs, such as, "Try to Remember" and "Misty," at every possible opportunity.

Qualified students with their own instruments may join the Mount Merry Symphony Orchestra which specializes in masterpieces of dentist office and elevator music. Tapes of the symphony orchestra's performances are heard on the phone whenever callers are put on hold by the administrative office.

The Pep Band, consisting solely of percussion instruments, is active on those infrequent occasions when there is sufficient student interest, and the Mount Merry Marching Band recruits all students who are able to carry an instrument and walk at the same time.

In addition to these on-campus events, the Waterbury area offers a number of establishments where recorded music is available for listening. Benny's Grill, in particular, is known for its especially good jukebox.

DRAMA

Mount Merry students may participate in the active student drama club, Greasepaint and Cold Cream, headed by faculty adviser Gretchen Indigo. Every year the club stages two productions in the recently completed Charo Auditorium. In the fall, the students produce a serious play, *Pygmalion,* and in the spring a musical, *My Fair Lady.* The club is open to all students and offers valuable experience in all aspects of theater: acting, directing, designing, costuming, lighting, stagecraft, promotion, ushering, sweeping, and popcorn vending.

DANCE

Mount Merry provides ample opportunities for dance enthusiasts with its wide-ranging dance programs. Prof. Gretchen Indigo conducts an exotic folk dancing series wherein students "tour" the world through the native dances of foreign countries. Many students have remarked that Professor Indigo's classes have stressed the universality of dance by revealing how many of them consist primarily of standing in a circle and clapping.

Another far more popular program in socio-ethnic dance is taught by Mr. LeRoi Paxton. Mr. Paxton instructs students in the up-to-the-minute trends in this field and emphasizes such significant points as choice of clothing, ways of acquiring a dance partner, and communicating through dance forms. His classes are always well attended and he personally supervises the selection of tunes for the jukebox at Benny's Grill where the class is held. Some of Mr. Paxton's students have gone on to appear on television on "Soul Train" and "Dance Fever."

For students who want a "serious" study of dance, Prof. Mary Dyche is happy to enroll them in her Modern Dance Seminar. An advocate of the Martha Graham School, Professor Dyche has personally choreographed many moving tone poems that her students perform each year. Her winter production is "Eliza's Flight Across the Ice Floes," performed on the Naugatuck River. In the spring, she presents her "Bacchae," danced by her female students and members of the nearby Waterbury Male Correctional Institute.

RADIO AND TELEVISION

Mount Merry owns and operates its own radio station, WONK, for student use. Under the guidance of faculty adviser Prof. Irving Klupferberg, students plan and program the station's broadcasts. Perennially favorite shows include: "Chess and Computer Quiz-Off," a call-in show that allows listeners (mainly from the Fernquist Math Center) to phone in and swap tricky chess moves and computer puzzles; "Talk About Sports!," a sports roundup that allows budding sportscasters to discuss, dissect, evaluate, re-evaluate, and, in general, babble on about every play in recent college sports tournaments; "The Dead Beat," a concert series devoted to the works of the Grateful Dead; and Kingston Mildew's "Masterpieces of Classical Music," a series of symphonic classics hosted by the veteran professor that airs every day from 2:00 A.M. to 6:00 A.M. except for the crucial weekend evenings of Saturday, Friday, and Thursday when the popular "Party Time Tunes" airs instead.

The school's closed-circuit cable system is available for interested students. Faculty adviser Prof. Bruno Coxman is responsible for the uncensored programming that can be seen in the

Mount Merry's Marching Band adds a lot of pep to athletic events.

PHOTO BUG

biology lab, several of the residence halls, and has been sold to the Escapade pay-TV network, which amply rewards the school for this service.

METEOROLOGY
The Meteorology Club meets on every occasion that there is a change of weather. Club members note the changes on a bulletin board in the Student Union and then plan what to wear on the basis of the current conditions. While open to all students, prospective members should be forewarned that they are responsible for their own gear and the club adviser, Prof. Caspar Q. Wimpley, is not responsible for missing or stolen umbrellas, rubbers, etc. Any student who extracts revenge on the adviser will be asked to leave the club, in a nice way.

FOREIGN HOUSE
The Foreign House is Mount Merry's own United Nations, and fosters a similar spirit of brotherhood. A student who elects to reside there must choose a foreign country (Puerto Rico doesn't count) and then adapt to that country's language, sleeping, eating, and bathroom habits. The house is equipped with a Jacuzzi, a Turkish bath, an Expresso machine, a bidet, and a bed of nails. The Foreign House is intended to give students a taste of life as foreigners see it, and to encourage international relations.

LIBRARY CLUB
The Library Club is led by the school librarian, Violet Bluestocking, and provides students with an invaluable glimpse into the intricacies of library science. "Like it says, it's a science!" Miss Bluestocking tells club members at their first meeting, and for the rest of the school year, members learn exactly what she means. A complete regimen of cataloging, filing, and shelving books, arranging periodicals, and collecting fines for overdue books at any cost is drawn up by Miss Bluestocking and students follow it down to the last letter of the Dewey decimal classification (Miss Bluestocking has eschewed the trendy Library of Congress system; "Too much trouble to change all those books," she has wisely noted). Based on the principle that the students should be able to maintain a library themselves, Miss Bluestocking sees to it that the Library Club gives them a chance to.

UNDERGRADUATES FOR GOD IN THE HUMANITIES (UGH)
UGH is an ecumenical organization of students who wish, in their lives and studies, to spread the Good News of the Christian faith. Although membership in UGH is not barred to students of the sciences, UGH believes that the humanities (especially of the pre-Darwinian period) are more conducive to systematic examination in a Christian light.

UGH members, insofar as faculty cooperation allows, do all their research projects on Christian topics and present these projects to the twice-weekly three-hour UGH meetings. The order of these meetings also includes lengthy Bible readings, exhaustive discussion, and at least half an hour of speaking in tongues.

The members of UGH, despite their ethnic and socio-economic diversity, can be easily identified on campus by their leather sandals and denim-covered Bibles. Through a program of extensive "witnessing" (which usually includes knocking on students' doors to read selected passages of Scripture at 3 A.M.), UGH continually seeks to swell its ranks.

The UGH outreach program extends to Waterbury and its surrounds as well—UGH students are often seen chatting enthusiastically with new friends on street corners. The annual UGH fund drive (during which members sell crucifixes hand-carved out of Ivory soap) nets sums of money about which the IRS is very curious.

PROTESTANT CLUB
The Protestant Club was formed by Lord Pennylacking on his arrival at Mount Merry as a genteel way for students of similar cultural backgrounds to meet and spend time together without apologizing for it. Though membership is open to all Protestants at Mount Merry, candidates must submit to interviews with the Governing Board of Alumni of the Protestant Club and Lord Pennylacking's formidable maiden aunts, in addition to producing letters of recommendation from at least two clergymen, one of whom should be either a bishop or English.

Protestant Club activities center around afternoon tea at Lord Pennylacking's house, accompanied by frequent readings of Oscar Wilde's *The Importance of Being Earnest* and Noel Coward's *Private Lives*. Annual events include a croquet tournament held in May and a

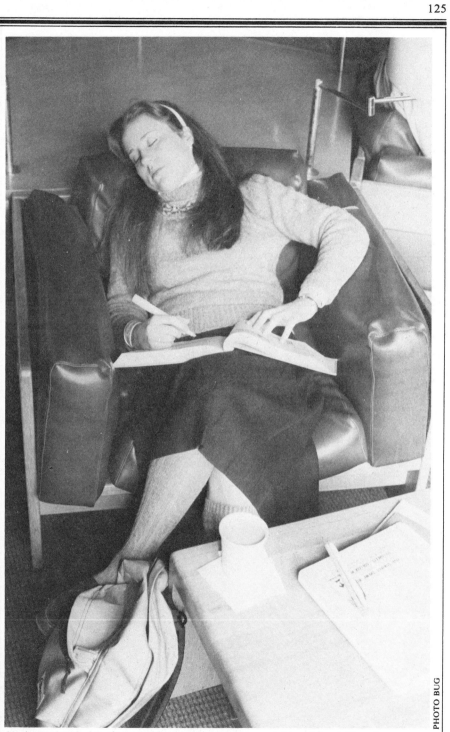

Students absorbed in the joy of learning are a common sight on Mount Merry's campus.

PHOTO BUG

Here comes the Peripatetic Club, back from another stroll!

wassail party held in December. The latter festival is especially enjoyable when membership in the Protestant Club climbs to more than three students and carols can be sung without embarrassment.

FRIENDS OF STUDENT DEVELOPMENT

Friends of Student Development is a group of well-meaning students which, along with the supportive faculty advisers, The O'Kays, sponsors a number of individual and group activities to assist students who seek either aid in personal growth or a way to kill time. These activities, which The O'Kays stress are "fun, as well as fundamental," include: assertiveness sessions (meets in the wrestling cage); leadership training (may get credit from the Speech Department); a Human Potential Seminar (motto: "I think I can, I think I can," etc.); time-management groups (covers increments of time from three minutes on up); problem-solving programs (how to stretch your budget with Green Stamps); hygiene awareness (what it means when all those blisters pop up on your . . .); and any other areas where individuals may need help, such as proper conduct during judicial hearings. These festive get-togethers are held at The O'Kays's farm where refreshments include The O'Kays's famous brownies.

STUDENT COUNCIL FOR AFFAIRS

The Student Council for Affairs takes responsibility for bringing culture to campus by importing amenable speakers and performers to Mount Merry. In your four or more years at Mount Merry you might witness such spectacles as an improvisational blind mime troupe, a handgun demonstration by a representative from the National Rifle Association, the North American Third World Theater Company's production of *Design for Living*, and Earl Butz.

Nevertheless, the Student Council for Affairs achieves its full potential with its elaborate party schedule. Events ranging from the heavily-attended weekly TGIF parties to the extravaganzas of each class's proms held on four consecutive weekends in May prove definitively that the council is the most important organization on campus.

SPORTS

Yet another facet of Mount Merry's dynamic progressiveness is manifested in its comprehensive four-year physical education plan. As the attention of the nation turns to physical fitness, Mount Merry's foresightedness in stressing physical activity is revealed. Students are required to participate in sports during all their years at Mount Merry, achieving the following benefits:

1. fulfillment of individual potential
2. skill and mastery
3. fitness
4. socio-cultural values

Students who are capable will be expected to play on a varsity team. Mount Merry fields teams in football, basketball, baseball, lacrosse, track, billiards, crew, and curling. Because the college belongs to no league, these varsity teams compete against each other—the match between the crew and the football team is one of the most spectacular events of the school year.

For students who are less competitive or competent, Mount Merry offers a number of athletic clubs by which they can satisfy the physical education requirement. These include bridge, bowling, checkers, pinball, kayaking, arm wrestling, roller disco, camping, fishing, darts, and the most popular of all, the Peripatetic Club with its Canine Auxiliary.

Sports facilities include a low-maintenance playing field, Fauntleroy Pond, Professor Beery's pool table, and the game room at the Student Union. The stable facilities include box stalls for Flicka, Misty, and the chairhorse of the Biology Department, Mr. Ed. Mount Merry rents from Waterbury institutions facilities such as rocks for rock-climbing and snow for snowshoeing.

The high point of the year's athletic events is the annual varsity and intramural awards night, at which hundreds of awards are given to athletes, athletic directors, officials, managers, water boys, equipment managers, cheerleaders, trainers, referees, and bench warmers.

There's always plenty to look at in Downing Beery's mass communications lectures.

WHAT DO I HAVE TO DO TO GET IN?

BECAUSE MOUNT MERRY PROVIDES a wide range of opportunities, activities and diversions, she appeals to a variety of students of vastly different temperaments, abilities, and backgrounds. The Admissions Office seeks to identify students who will enjoy the numerous pleasures and satisfactions Mount Merry has to offer. In addition to academic data, an applicant's motivation and desire to attend Mount Merry are taken into account, especially if they are dramatically and graphically demonstrated. Mount Merry attempts to accommodate every candidate regardless of his degree of readiness for college. The Admissions Office considers every candidate without regard to race, ethnic origin, weight, color, tan, creed, age, or any physical or mental impairment.

WHO MAY APPLY

Mount Merry welcomes applications from anybody with $100 for the non-refundable applications fee and an envelope with a 20¢ stamp. Mount Merry has a policy of nondiscrimination on the basis of race, religion, age, sex, handicap, or ancestry.

HOW TO APPLY

An application is included at the rear of this catalog. Duplicate application forms, as needed, are available by writing or telephoning the Admissions Office.

INFORMATION ON ARRANGING VISITS AND TOURS OF THE SCHOOL

Due to the flood of applications Mount Merry receives, the Admissions Office discourages personal visits because she's overworked as it is. Moreover, this catalog contains many pictures of the campus and students that should tell you all you need to know. If you insist on visiting Mount Merry, please do not arrive unannounced.

HOW TO COMMUNICATE WITH MOUNT MERRY

Please direct all telephone correspondence to the Mount Merry switchboard. Be prepared to leave your name, number, and message on the tape and someone will try to get back to you.

ADMISSION REQUIREMENTS

1. $100 non-refundable application fee. Make checks payable to School Comptroller Izzy A. Shyster.

2. Demonstrated ability to write and speak correct, grammatical English.

3. Completion of a high school education as certified by a diploma in the applicant's name or a transcript or other convincing record of attendance. In the absence of a high school record, students must present the results of Mount Merry's Competency Test, which is administered to them by their parents. The test does not include a self-addressed stamped envelope—mailing it back to the college is part of the examination.

4. Recommendations from a high school or elementary school faculty member or baby sitter. (It is suggested that in order to obtain these recommendations, students become well known to certain faculty members in honorable and unobtrusive ways. Unusual originality, insight, and energy are very impressive; so are gifts.)

5. Completion of at least the minimum subject requirements shown below:

4 credits physical education
4 credits English
1 credit algebra
1 credit other math
1 credit foreign language
1 credit natural science
1 credit history
1 credit shop
(Strict adherence to this minimum may be waived by the Admissions Office in consideration of other contributions.)

NOTE: Candidates for the B.S. in Ranology must apply directly to Reuben Dingleberry, whose criteria for admission are somewhat more rigorous and change with every new advance in the dynamic field of Frog Studies.

STANDARDIZED TESTS

Results of the SAT (Scholastic Aptitude Test), ACT (American College Test), TOEFL (Test of English as a Foreign Language), ECT (English Composition Test), and Achievement Test, or any other test administered by CEEB (College Entrance Examination Board) or ETS (Educational Testing Service) may be offered to the admissions board, which may or may not pay attention.

EARLY DECISION

Well-endowed or otherwise qualified candidates who have selected Mount Merry as their only hope are encouraged to apply for an early decision. This plan is designed to single out the students who have come to the conclusion that Mount Merry is the only place for them. In the case of the early decision application, the candidate agrees to apply to no other colleges until hearing from Mount Merry (via collect phone call). If admitted, he is obligated to attend Mount Merry or negotiate a settlement with School Comptroller Izzy A. Shyster. (In the event of court action, the candidate will be held responsible for the college's attorney's fees.)

TRANSFER STUDENTS

Mount Merry frequently appeals to transfer students who have not found a niche for themselves, academic or social, at their previous colleges. Students interested in transferring to Mount Merry must submit the following:
    1. An application for admission including the non-refundable application fee based on class: Sophomores $100, Juniors $200, Seniors $300;
    2. Grades from the last semester at the previous institution, whether the semester's course work was finished or not;
    3. Copy of catalog of college attended or other proof that such a college exists;
    4. Certification from the college's dean that the student has paid all debts at the college and no litigation is pending against him;
    5. A statement from the applicant explaining why the transfer is necessary.

DEADLINES FOR APPLICATION

Apply early! Because Mount Merry has a rolling admissions policy, you are notified of your acceptance a mere six weeks after your application is received. This gives early applicants the luxury of enjoying their senior year of high school free from worry about where they'll go to college. You may apply at any time between the beginning of your senior year in high school and a month before the beginning of the Mount Merry term. It is preferred by the administration that you apply *before* registering for classes.

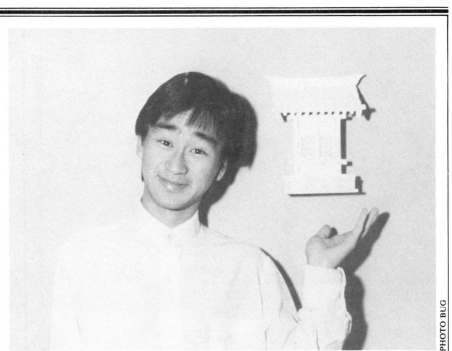

PHOTO BUG

Professor Doo Wop shares his knowledge about Oriental living conditions.

Natasha Goldman at a popular fund-raiser for the Women Faculty's Coalition Splinter Group.

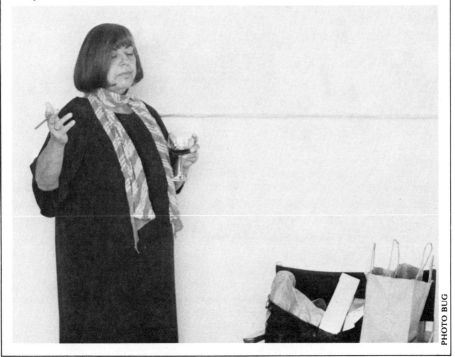

PHOTO BUG

PHOTO BUG

Lambert Glibb will stop at nothing to make a point.

HOW MUCH DO I HAVE TO PAY?

Mount Merry prides herself on her capacity to provide her students with a quality education despite the absence of an endowment. Unlike other colleges which depend on alumni or institutional support, Mount Merry relies solely on tuition and other fees paid by her students. Although Mount Merry's tuition may seem comparatively high, it enables the college to offer its unique brand of education.

Fees must be paid in full for the entire school year by August 1. No place will be held for a student after August 1 if the entire year's fees are not paid in full. Students who do not pay by then must find replacements to fill their places.

If conditions should make such a change necessary, Mount Merry reserves the right to increase its fees at any point in the term and to bill students for immediate payment of the difference, retroactive to the student's acceptance to Mount Merry.

FEES

Comprehensive Fee—full academic year	$15,000.00
(10% discount for students sixty-five or over)	
Tuition	$ 6,000.00
Room	$ 4,000.00 (while classes are in session)
Board	$ 4,000.00
Teachers' salaries	$ 120.00 a week
Plant maintenance	$ 250.00
Installments on Dr. Kaiser's Bentley	$ 300.00 monthly
Books and supplies	$ 1.50
Personal expenses	$ 3,000.00

MISCELLANEOUS EXPENSES

ID card	$ 3.00
Altered ID card	$ 6.00
Bicycle registration	$ 6.00
Tricycle registration	$ 9.00
Wheelchair registration	$ 12.00
Check-bouncing charge	$ 15.00 each
Spouse activity card	$ 5.00 each
Pet activity card	$ 10.00 per leg
Linen service	$ 25.00
Clean linen service	$ 50.00
Student Activities Fee (Beer)	$ 100.00
Campus Family Planning Center Warehouse Fee	$ 125.00

SPORTS FEES

Swimming Test	$ 30.00
Passing grade on Swimming Test	$ 50.00
Equipment rentals	
Bowling balls (for use in alley)	$ 5.00
Bowling balls (for use outside of alley)	$ 10.00

Gretchen Indigo, highly sensitive to all the beauty in the world, makes a practice of conducting all her classes outdoors.

Anthropology students learn the value of found objects.

Misty	$	8.00
Flicka	$	16.00
Crew (oar)	$	12.00
Crew (lake)	$	24.00
Jockstrap		.50

ART AND MUSIC FEES

Clay rental	$	5.00
Model fee	$	80.00 an hour
Use of practice room for piano	$	5.00 per hour
Use of piano	$	10.00 per hour
Use of organ for practice	$	25.00 per half hour
Recital fee	$	8.00
Audience for recital	$	1.50 per head

INSURANCE PLAN
All students are required to subscribe to the Mount Merry life insurance plan, naming School Comptroller Izzy A. Shyster as their beneficiary.

FINANCIAL AID

Mount Merry discourages applications for financial aid, maintaining that students who can't pay for college have no business applying in the first place. Candidates for admission should note that application for financial aid could seriously reduce their chances of being admitted to the college. Financial aid at Mount Merry, skimpy though it is, takes the following forms:

SCHOLARSHIPS
A few scholarships are available to qualified students who are willing to follow the prescribed courses of study. The Florence Hyman Scholarship awards $1,200 to the female student from Iowa who shows promise in getting those tough stains out of polyester, acetate, and spandex garments. The Ralph Oxenwald Athletic Scholarship, established by Mount Merry's most famous athlete who constituted the entire defensive line of the school's football team from 1938–46, awards a full scholarship for an unlimited number of years to the largest applicant of either sex. The oldest scholarship at Mount Merry is the Aural Rupert Religious Vocation Scholarship, founded in 1894 to provide an education for a student who, after graduation, plans to go to Africa and take up a missionary position.

WORK-STUDY
Work-study programs are offered to financial aid applicants who weren't lucky enough to get a scholarship. Students help pay for their tuition by working on campus in such capacities as garbage man, handyman, dishwasher, roofer, mechanic, exterminator, and general maintenance crew. Program overseer Prof. Mary Dyche reviews and evaluates students' output on a regular basis.

Mount Merry also makes every effort to help students find employment in Waterbury by making available the want ads from the local paper and by pointing out the most lucrative corner for street musicians.

PHOTO BUG

Another Geology field project.

WHO RUNS THIS SCHOOL?

ADMINISTRATION:

Chaplain: Dr. Reginald Kaiser
Chancellor: Dr. Vonetta Fitzcox
Vice-President for Academic Affairs: Johann Junker
Vice-President for Student Affairs: Buddy Upson
Admissions Director: Dottie Pringle
Vice-President for Ranology: Newt Pickerel
School Comptroller: Izzy A. Shyster
Registrar: Rosemary Hardboiled
Bursar: Cary Nichols

THE OFFICE OF THE DEANS:

Dean Paul Martin
Dean Jones
Dean Martin
John Dean

Dean Rusk
Jan & Dean
Dean Acheson
Deanna Durbin

THE REGENTS:

Anointed Regent: Francis Xavier Milligan, S.J.
Regent Ex Officio: Francis Xavier Mulligan, S.J.
Regent Designate: Francis Xavier Flanagan, S.J.
Regent in Training: Francis Xavier Murphy, S.J.

STAFF:

Assistant for Community Relations: Roy C. Coney
   (also College Legal Counsel, Student Legal Counsel)
Librarian: Violet Bluestocking
Superintendent for Buildings and Grounds: Orlando Jesus Garcia
Director of Public Safety and Campus Traffic: Leon De Thugg
Textbook Buyer: Esther Wellred
Manager, Kampus Korner Kanteen: Bertha Butt
Chief of Security: Martin Nett
Duplicating Office and Mailroom: Willie Lee String
Food Services: Dinah N. Kitchen
   (also Veterinary Services)
Nurse: Aurelia Slouch
Consulting Psychiatrist: Dr. Alexander Lucre
Career Planning Counselor: Arnold Botcher
Fines Monitor: Larry Graft
Director, International Student Services: Kyril Wycŏgnskrïnskøvic
Office for Sexual Harassment: Hans Orff

PHOTO BUG

Turn here to get to Mount Merry.

HOW DO I GET THERE?

WATERBURY IS LOCATED IN central Connecticut at the intersection of I-84 and Route 8 on the scenic Naugatuck River. The easiest way to reach Mount Merry is by car. Any other way, you're on your own.

From I-84, exit from the thruway at the Holy Land exit and take a right directly under the highway, drive five or six blocks until you pass a shopping center with an A&P in it. The second or third right should be Injun Hill Road (if you get to the Dunkin' Donuts, you've gone too far). Take Injun Hill Road until you get to a fork where you sort of bear left, between the sycamore trees, and you'll be on Snake Pit Road. Drive for ⅜ of a mile and the entrance to the campus will be approximately one hundred yards away.

OR

From Route 8, exit at Squamtuk Avenue exit and then take a right until you're heading toward the big cross on the hill at Holy Land (you can't miss it). Go straight for a while even though the road curves around. Keep going. When you get to Vincent's Furniture Shoppe (with the painted sign on the side) turn left and you'll be on Samarusmitnick Road. Drive 50 yards and then start looking for signs saying "Mount Merry College—Service Entrance." Turn right at the trash cans and the driveway to the campus is on your left.

PHOTO BUG

PHOTO BUG

School Comptroller Izzy A. Shyster.

FACULTY

Norman Bates, B.A., Reed College; McLean Hospital; Institut des Etudes Psychologiques, Geneva. Chairman, Psychology Department. (Social Deviants; Genetics; Greek Tragedy; Artificial Intelligence; Logic; Motivation; Perception and Cognition; Getting Rid of Your Accent; Dream Analysis)

Mr. Bates has a special interest in the so-called "fringe" aspects of human behavior and mental health. He lives alone in a large house out in the country with his pet rat.

Downing Beery, B.A., Dartmouth College. Chairman, Mass Communications Department. (Residual Effects of Alcohol on the Human Body; Risk Management; Ancient Comic Traditions; Classical Mythology; Radio Announcing; Physics for Dilettantes; Religious Stereotypes; Beach and Island Geological Processes; Roman Civilization; Probability; Music in White American Culture)

Mr. Berry buys all his clothes at Brooks Brothers and deeply regrets the advent of coeducation at Dartmouth. He has taught at Mount Merry for thirty years and has learned no new jokes in that time.

Reverend Bruce Cademyte, B.A., Columbia College; M. Div., General Theological Seminary. Chairman, Classics Department. (Political Theory and Practice in Ancient Rome; Church Latin; American Decorative Arts; Homological Algebra; Greek Philosophy; Fluids, Waves, and Heat; Introduction to China; Principles of Paleontology; Meat Appreciation; Women and Antiquity; the Lyric Voice; Oral Communication)

Reverend Cademyte is an ordained minister in the Episcopal church, with extremely high-church leanings. He left his last parish after an argument with the bishop about the use of incense at Morning Prayer. Reverend Cademyte is well known at Mount Merry for his taste for the finer things of life; he lives on campus in the former Lady Chapel, which he has decorated with Spanish devotional paintings.

PHOTO BUG

PHOTO BUG

PHOTO BUG

Sister Consuela Concepción Immaculata Dónde esta el Lavatorio, B.A., Universidad de Tijuana. (Elementary Spanish, Spanish Culture, Gypsy Studies)

Sister Consuela appeared on campus one rainy night and has been here ever since. She immediately assumed a position in the formerly nonexistent Spanish division of the Foreign Languages Department, as Spanish is her only tongue. Owing to her natural reticence and abnormal secretiveness (in addition to her inability to speak English), little else is known about Sister Consuela. Her striking resemblance to Father Savonarola, however, has often been remarked upon.

Bruno Coxman, B.A., U.C.L.A. Chairman, Philosophy Department. (Playboy Philosophy; Applied Sexuality; Sex Stratification and the Social Experience of Men; Sensations; Personality and Social Relations; Interpersonal Sexuality; Symbolism; Body Language; Video; Our Bodies, Our Selves)

Mr. Coxman's broad experience in his field is matched by the enthusiasm, energy, and staying power that made him successful in his previous careers as model and escort.

Leon De Thugg, Jake LaMotta School of Defense. Chairman, Speech Department. (Self-Defense; Action Speaks Louder than Words; Visual Patterns in Nature; Socio-Economic Policy; Student Teaching in Waterbury; Law and the Resourceful Criminal; Mechanics; Sociology of Imprisonment; Delinquency and Gangs in School and Society; Sport Strategies and Techniques)

Mr. De Thugg's career is unique among Mount Merry's faculty. Formerly a bodyguard for a Filipino diplomat, he turned his talents to free-lance operations when his former employer died. He comes to Mount Merry from the New York City Department of Corrections.

CAMERA SHY

PHOTO BUG

PHOTO BUG

Steve E. Dore, Co-chairperson (male), Physical Education Department. (Health and Hygiene; Sleep and Fitness; Advanced Computer Systems; Economics and Sports; History of Leisure in America; Media Coverage of Sports; Athletic Officiating I; Athletic Officiating II; Giants of Physical Thought)

Mr. Dore is virtually uneducated and the level of his IQ is apparently very low. However, his physical capabilities, calm temperament, and deep voice give him great advantages in his chosen field.

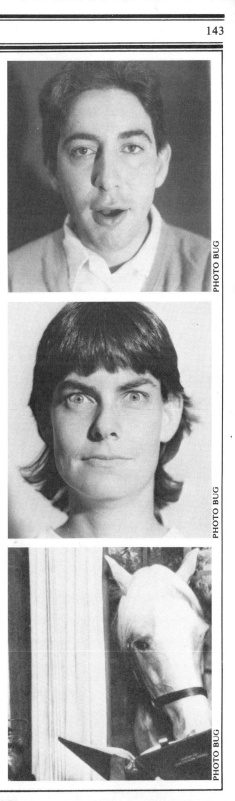

Mary Dyche, B.A., Trenton State College. Co-chairperson (female), Physical Education Department. (Body Building and Slenderizing; Body Image and the Aesthetic Experience; Human Potential; Grading; Theories in Physical Education; Latin American Social Dancing; Biochemistry and Weight Loss)

Ms. Dyche's enjoyment of active sports is well known on the Mount Merry campus, and her coaching methods (which owe much to the "hurt-pain-agony" training philosophy) are famous all over Waterbury. She is also known for her staging of the commencement exercises, which last year included 150 sit-ups and a human pyramid by the graduating class.

Mr. Ed, Chairhorse, Biology Department. (Equine Science)

Mr. Ed, who has gained wide exposure for his articulateness in the field of equine-human relations, brings a unique advantage to his teaching of Equine Science. He lives on campus in a large converted stable with Flicka and Misty. He has won numerous awards, including blue ribbons and the Patsy Award.

PHOTO BUG

PHOTO BUG

PHOTO BUG

Irma Feeley, A.A., Finch College. (The Male Nude; Personality and Social Relations; Sensations; Romantic Latin Tradition; Computers in Psychology; Interpersonal Sexuality; Love in Eastern Cultures; Elementary Conversational French; Meat Appreciation; Oral Communication; The Concubine as Policymaker; Our Bodies, Our Selves)

Although Ms. Feeley's academic experience ended after two years of college, her informal—even intimate—education continues. Despite her heavy course load, she keeps marathon office hours, motivated by her voracious appetite and her ongoing search for scholastic stimulation.

Mr. Joe Franklin, Chairman, Physics Department. (Descriptive Astronomy)

Mr. Franklin has been a major force in stargazing for over twenty years. His late-night academic program includes a galaxy of luminaries and others. He has published his research in *Joe Franklin's Memory Lane News,* which enjoys a large following.

Procter Gamble, B.S., Texas Police Academy; Our Lady of Perpetual Help Business School. Chairman, Mathematics Department. (Chemistry in Action; Introductory Biology; Dull Normal Mathematics; Deviance and Social Control)

Mr. Gamble has always had a deep respect for the law and its severe beauty. The high point of his life was his long-ago four-day membership in the motorcycle brigade of the Los Angeles Police Force. His deep interest in formations and order led him to the field of mathematics, and he further expresses those interests by his leadership of Mount Merry's Marching Band, and his captaincy of all fire drills.

PHOTO BUG

PHOTO BUG

PHOTO BUG

Lambert Glibb, B.S., Babson College. Chairman, Economics Department. (Introduction to Advertising; Changing Africa; Anthropology of Tourism; Planning and Projection for the Future; Dollars and Cents; Personal Finance; Modern American Novel; Creative Writing: Very Famous American Writers: Law and the Social Sanction; How to Get Published; Popular Songwriting and Arranging; Advanced Persuasion)

Mr. Glibb's position in the world of media is attested to by his career path; he has moved from the large advertising firm of Thin Air to the "boutique" of Gargle and Guano, to his own public relations firm, Lambert Glibb, P.C. He has helped many Mount Merry students place their feet on the bottom rung of the ladder to success.

Natasha Goldman, B.A., Mount Holyoke; M.B.A., Harvard University; Ph.D., University of Chicago. Carrie Nation Professor of Women's Studies. (Personnel Management; Female Development; Educational Psychology; Magic and Witchcraft; Domestic Contracts; Women in Media; Language and Interpretation; Introduction to American Politics; Hermeneutic Semantics; Sociology of the Family; Argumentation; "God": Fact or Fiction?)

Ms. Goldman is a member of NOW, Planned Parenthood, and Women Against Pornography. She was attracted to the former Carrie Nation Temperance College twenty-five years ago in the hopes of forming a Women's Studies Department. Formerly she taught at the University of Chicago, where she and her husband co-chaired the Home Economics Department until his departure for the University of Miami in the company of a blonde co-ed.

Col. Ulysses Hawk, United States Army, B.S., West Point; M.Ed., St. Lawrence University. Chairman, Politics Department. (Wars; Homeric War Correspondence; Leisure Evaluation and Counseling; Women's Role in the East; Soviet-type Economics; Great Books of Western Tradition; Latin American Politics)

Col. Hawk is a respected and venerated colonel in the U.S. Army who is held in awe by students and campus pets for his no-nonsense demeanor and autocratic temperament. His ever-present riding

PHOTO BUG

PHOTO BUG

PHOTO BUG

crop (which he has been known to wield with effective accuracy) is his trademark, along with his army jeep which is kept in mint condition by students needing academic assistance.

Gretchen Indigo, B.A., Bennington College; University of California at Santa Cruz. Chairman, Folklore Department. (Plant Biology; Marital Counseling Through Poetry; Modern Poetry; Implications of Folk Music; American Intellectual History Since 1975; International Relations; American Folk Dancing)

Ms. Indigo is highly sensitive to all the beauty in the world. She lives on a farm outside of town with her illegitimate son, Corduroy.

Reginald Kaiser, M.A., (Oxon.); Ph.D., Yale University. Chaplain of Mount Merry College. (History of Mount Merry College)

Dr. Kaiser has been Chaplain of Mount Merry College since 1943, so he has lived much of the history that he teaches in his famous History of Mount Merry College. His deep love for the college and his life-long dedication to its ideals give him such a reverence for the course material that his lectures have gone unchanged for nearly thirty years.

PHOTO BUG

Hildegarde Agnes Gertrude Klumpp, B.A., Carrie Nation Temperance College. Chairman, Home Economics Department. (Buying Behavior and Market Decisions; Problems in Eastern Gastronomy; Modern Economic Thought; Sedimentology; Food Chemistry; Laundry Problems; Home Economics Practicum; Market Policy; Gastronomical Geometry; Microwave Studies; Christian Marriage and Family)

Miss Klumpp, niece of the three Klumpp sisters who founded Carrie Nation Temperance College, was brought up by them after her own parents died, and took all three of their names in gratitude. As sole beneficiary of their wills, she is Trustee of the famous Klumpp Memorial Wing of the Art Center. She lives in the rec room on the classic 1950-vintage Murphy bed.

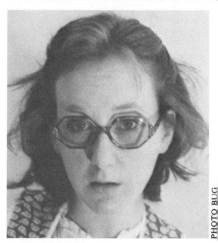
PHOTO BUG

Irving Klupferberg, B.S., N.Y.U.; Ph.D., Yeshiva; Ph.D., Ranology Center, Mount Merry College. Chairman, Computer Science Department. (Electronics; Sociology of the Possible; Anthropology and Modern Life; Erotic Nature; Structural Biochemistry; Electronic Circuits Lab; Yiddish for Gentiles; Transport History; Calculus; Statistical Physics; Fundamental Algorithms)

Mr. Klupferberg has been a prodigy all his life. He graduated from New York University at the age of fourteen, and by the age of eighteen had earned two Ph.D.s in very different subjects. He has a great affinity for computers and electronic games, and is well known on campus for his colorful collection of pocket pen guards.

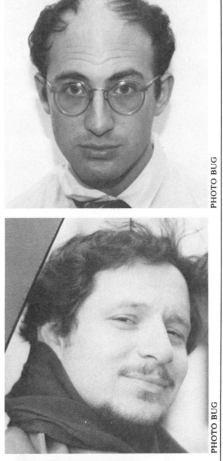

Frank Lloyd Kovalchick, B.A., Yale University; Ecole du Louvre; Famous Artists' School. Chairman, Art and Art History Department. (Problems in Modern American Architecture and Urban Planning; Creative Photography; Trends and Movements in Applied Aesthetics; Modern American Art; Conflict as Nuance in the Eastern Film; Stylistics; Remedial Television; Model Theory; Aesthetics; Epicureanism; Status and Power; Pop Muzik)

Mr. Kovalchick lived in Paris for three weeks, painting Neo-natalistic self-portraits in a Left Bank garret, before settling on Mount Merry's nourishing artistic atmosphere and financially protective environment. His skills as an appreciator are remarkable, and he takes pride in his methods for bringing "culture" to Mount Merry and Waterbury. He goes to New York on weekends and subscribes to *W* and *Interview.*

Pepe Le Pue, Certificat de Phonétique, Paris VII; License Ier degré de Langages, Montpellier; Berlitz School of Languages. Chairman, Foreign Languages Department. (Elementary Eastern Languages; The Language of Romance; Continental Philosophy; English as a Foreign Language; La Cuisine de France; Problems in Opera; France in Turmoil: 1789 to Today)

M. Le Pue, who is one hundred percent French, represents everything European to Mount Merry. He lives in the Foreign House, where his beret, bathing habits, and the empty wine bottles on his floor prove his Gallic authenticity.

Alexander Lucre, M.D., Psy. (What's Your Problem?)

Dr. Lucre very kindly takes time out from his busy Hartford psychiatric practice to lend his expertise to Mount Merry. Many of his past students have gone on to become valuable clients after graduation.

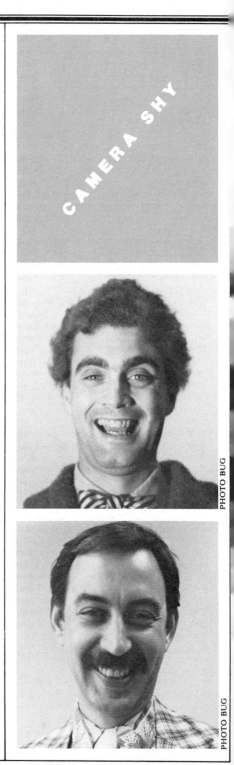

Earl E. Mann, B.A., Goddard College; Ph.D., Tanzania Tech. Chairman, Anthropology Department. (Practical Archaeology; Human Evolution; Greek and Latin Roots; Introduction to Geography; Occupations, Professions, and Careers)

Mr. Mann, after pursuing his Ph.D. energetically in Africa, brought his enthusiasm to Mount Merry, where he is constantly delving into the past, the present, and a few places where he doesn't belong at all. A proponent of the simple life, he lives in a hut on the site of the Waterbury Refuse Park, putting into practical use many of the household artifacts found there.

Hugo Markup, School of Hartt Knox, City Streets; Profitt Practical Study School of Merchandising. Chairman, Business Department. (Gemstones as Investment; Quantitative Methods; Entrepreneurial Studies; The Eastern Market; The Epic; Modern Drama; Petroleum and Its Implications; Atomic and Nuclear Physics; Ethics and the Professions; Investing in the Law)

Mr. Markup, more than anyone at Mount Merry, has a deep and realistic understanding of the capitalist system and how it functions in today's society. His apprenticeship on Seventh Avenue and Forty-seventh Street in New York and his many friends in the entertainment field ensure that his teaching is practical above all else.

Daisy McGillicuddy, A.B., Princeton University; M.B.A., J.D., Harvard University; LLD., Stanford University. Chairman, Legal Studies Department. (Citizens and the Law; Law Through Literature; Effects of Mass Media; First Amendment; Interest Groups, Lobbying, and the Political Process)

Ms. McGillicuddy, a firm proponent of affirmative action, often cites her own achievements to inspire students with the message that anyone can turn any circumstance to his own advantage. In addition to chairing the Legal Studies Department, Dr. McGillicuddy works as a paralegal at a prestigious Waterbury law firm.

Kingston Mildew, B.A., Harvard College; M. Div., Yale University; LLD., LittD., L.H.D., S.T.L., Cambridge University (England). Chairman, History Department. (Attic Greek; The Animal Kingdom; Theological English; Early Poetic Masters; Verbiage; Problems in Folk Tales and Legends; Future of New England's Mill Towns; Concepts of Existence; Presidents; Adulthood and Aging; Life in the Modern Church; Unsolved Problems; Masterpieces; The Bach Family; Dream Analysis)

Mr. Mildew is Mount Merry's oldest professor. His occasional absentmindedness in no way diminishes his great learning, and his constantly forgiving attitude toward his students makes his courses highly regarded, if ill-attended.

Sgt. Pat O'Brien (Police, Law, and Society) Sergeant O'Brien is a member of Waterbury's fine police force, where he enjoys the reputation of being the best shot at his precinct. Sgt. O'Brien is also well-known for his captaincy of the Clancy's Bar darts team, and for his warm six-year marriage during the course of which his wife has produced seven children (no twins).

PHOTO BUG

PHOTO BUG

CAMERA SHY

The O'Kays, B.A., Maharishi International University; Esalen Institute; Naropa Institute. Co-chairmen, Development Studies Department. (Personal Growth; Decision Making; Values Clarification; Ritual in Everyday Life; Religious Personalities; Group Thinking and Discussion)

The O'Kays are native Californians who met at a TM training center in Marin County and believe deeply in the essential Togetherness Potential of every soul. They meditate, jog, drink Perrier water, and take at least one trip per year to Big Sur. They live in a cooperative yurt on Gretchen Indigo's farm.

Harry Palmer, B.A., St. John's University (Minnesota). (Self-Abuse; Teaching Children's Literature; Organic Chemistry)

Mr. Palmer has devoted his academic career to a study of man's need for self-fulfillment and the methods by which he achieves it. He lives in a small mobile unit on campus and maintains a cottage to house his large research library. Mount Merry feels itself to be uniquely endowed with Mr. Palmer's talents at its fingertips.

LeRoi Paxton, B.A., Howard University. Chairman, Music Department. (Fundamentals of Jazz; Rhythm; Motifs in Afro-American Music)

A former member of the Temptations, Mr. Paxton first attracted the attention of the Mount Merry faculty when his band—The DeLuxites—performed at a school dance. Renowned for his dancing ability and white boots, Paxton is one of the school's most colorful and popular instructors.

PHOTO BUG

PHOTO BUG

PHOTO BUG

Earnest St. George Bredon Osbert, Lord Pennylacking, Eton College; M.A., (Oxon.). Chairman, Sociology Department. (Highbrow Media; Introduction to Discreet Mathematics; European Politics and Diplomacy; Social Change in Caribbean Society; Small Talk; Social Inequality; Social Position of Artists; Peasant Societies; Sociolinguistics; Status and Power; Wealth and Poverty in Greece and Rome; Brush Up Your Shakespeare; Advanced Conversation; European Society; Domestic Management)

Lord Pennylacking, eighteenth Baron of Ramshackle, left England upon the Duke of Windsor's abdication. His extreme sensitivity to class as manifested in dress, language, and behavior assures him that he is invited to all the right parties in Waterbury.

Newt Pickerel, B.S., Bayou State College; Ph.D., University of the Amazon, Brazil. (Elementary Frog Studies).

Dr. Pickerel, perhaps the outstanding Ranology scholar in northwestern Connecticut, whose very name is synonomous with frog studies, condescends to teach Mount Merry's undergraduates. His empathetic approach to frogs results in his innovative teaching methods, notably his terrarium classroom where students squat for the duration of his taped lectures. Dr. Pickerel's best known opus is his recording of mating calls of *Rana pipiens* which is broadcast daily at noon on WONK.

Major Pusher B.A., University of California at Berkeley; M.S., Instituto de Cannabis, Colombia. (The Works of Carlos Castaneda; Ethnobotany; Historical Geology; Chemistry in Literature)

Mr. Pusher's mellow attitude toward life is only one of the characteristics that makes him a very popular figure on campus. At any hour his caretaker's cottage (where he has cultivated a flourishing market garden) is a beehive of activity. His frequent trips to South America keep him abreast of the most recent developments in his field(s).

PHOTO BUG

PHOTO BUG

CAMERA SHY

Mrs. Rogers, Chairman, Education Department. (Communicating with Preschoolers; Introduction to Arts and Crafts; Color in Art; Basic Human Anatomy; Computers and You; Individual Differences in Children; Adult Education; Elementary Composition; Meet the Integers; Interrogative Mode; Psychological Testing)

Mrs. Rogers's simple approach to learning and her confiding manner make her the ideal teacher for most Mount Merry students.

Rob Rush, B.A., University of California at Berkeley; Ph.D., Institut der Physiopharmakologie, Hamburg. Chairman, Chemistry Department. (Recreational Chemistry; Stress; States of Consciousness)

Mr. Rush was deeply influenced by the teachings of Timothy Leary and by certain of Sigmund Freud's precepts. He feels that men should take advantage of every benefit of the modern age in order to make their lives more colorful, thrilling, or even simply to get to sleep at night.

Rev. Moses Savonarola, S.J., S.T.B., Loyola University; M. Div., Jesuit School of Theology; S.T.D., Pontifical Gregorian University. Chairman, Religion and Theology Department. (Legal and Moral Responsibility; Economics and Religion; Choir; Ethics; Gospel According to Hollywood; Grace and Sin; Platonic Philosophy)

Rev. Savonarola regards himself as the custodian of the souls of Mount Merry's faculty and students, a responsibility he takes very seriously. When not teaching or hearing confession, he can be found in his cell in the basement of the chapel, wearing a hair shirt.

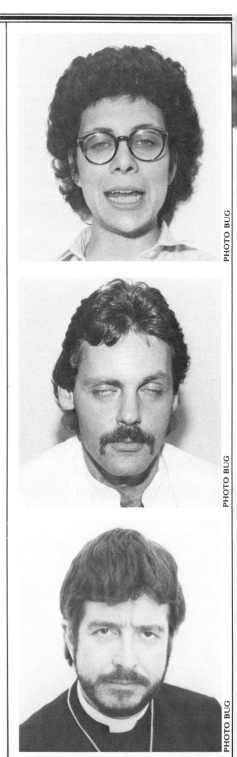

PHOTO BUG

PHOTO BUG

PHOTO BUG

Izzy A. Shyster, Self-taught. (Tax-Free Gifts)

Mr. Shyster, who serves ably as the School Comptroller, is also a noted local contractor. He claims proudly that he has had a hand in building and maintaining nearly every edifice on campus. His influence is equally widely felt all over Waterbury. His other interests include liquor wholesaling and legalized gambling in Connecticut.

PHOTO BUG

Verna, Visiting Professor with the Rank of Lecturer. (Elementary Cashiering)

Verna is a crack cashier; after graduation from the Cashier Training Institute, she has been employed at various branches of Stop&Shop, Grand Union, and Medi-Mart.

CAMERA SHY

Storm E. Wether, B.A., Mount Merry College. Chairman, Geology Department. (Weather; Geology Survey)

The only native son on Mount Merry's faculty, Storm E. Wether has been deeply influenced by School Comptroller Izzy A. Shyster. From his earliest youth in Waterbury, he has been deeply interested in the use of lands and development patterns, and is now applying his knowledge of geology to the benefit of Mount Merry students, School Comptroller Izzy A. Shyster, and himself.

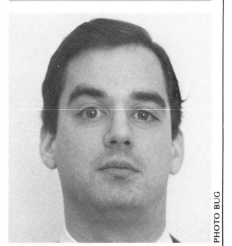

PHOTO BUG

Caspar Q. Wimpley, B.A., Hamilton College. Chairman, English Department. (First Aid; English I; Proofreading; Introduction to Mass Media; Listening to Music; Fundamentals of Laboratory Measurement; Research Methods; English Training Camp; Coordinating Seminar; Business Communication; Chemistry for the Liberal Arts; Numerical Analysis with a Programmable Calculator; Methods and Materials; Teaching Health in Elementary School; Xerography; Art of the Sentence)

Mr. Wimpley's great strength is his deep grasp of administrative and organizational problems and his knowledge of the functional aids available through most stationery stores. Mr. Wimpley devotes his spare time to inventions like a collapsible filing cabinet.

Doo Wop, B.A., Confucius College; Ph.D., Floating University. Chairman, Eastern Studies Department. (Basic Eastern Studies; Introduction to Philosophical Theory; Eastern Philosophy; Left, Right, and Center; From Marx to Mao; Byzantine History)

Mr. Wop, who was brought up and educated in mainland China, joined Mount Merry's faculty last year. Although his command of English is not firm and he has yet to grasp the significance of grades, he seems to be adjusting nicely.

PHOTO BUG

PHOTO BUG

APPLICATION FORM

NOTE: Legible Handwriting Preferred

1. Have you included your $100 non refundable application fee? Yes _____

2. Name _____ (first) _____ (middle) _____ (last)

   Nickname(s) _____, _____, _____

   Other aliases _____, _____, _____

3. Have you ever applied to Mount Merry before? Yes, in 19____, in 19____, in 19____,
   Can't remember _____

4. Proposed date of entry: _____

5. When do you expect to come: _____

6. Do you wish to be considered for Financial Aid?
   No ___ Yes ___ (if yes, complete no more of this application)

7. Marital Status: Married Once ___ Married Twice ___ Married Three or More ___
   Widowed ___ Divorced ___ Separated ___ Single ___ Stalling ___

8. Schools attended in the last 5 years: _____
   _____
   _____
   _____
   _____
   _____

9. If you haven't been in school for the past 5 years, would you mind telling us what you *have*
   been doing?

   "Oh, just _____ ."

10. Ethnic or Racial Affiliation:
    ___ American Indian/Alaskan Native   ___ Philippine/Filipino
        (include tribal affiliation)   ___ Chinese/Chinese-American
    ___ Black/Afro-American   ___ East Indian/Pakistani
    ___ Chicano/Mexican-American   ___ Japanese/Japanese-American
    ___ Latino/Other Spanish-American   ___ Korean
    ___ White/Euro-American   ___ Polynesian
    ___ White Russian   ___ Other Asian (specify)
    ___ Aleutian

11. Are you a U.S. Citizen: Yes ___ No ___
    If not a citizen, are you a refugee? ___ An illegal alien? ___ Any kind of alien? ___

12. Are you a member of the Communist Party? _____

13. Have you ever served part or all of a sentence at a correctional
    or penal institution?   Yes ___ No ___
    Have you ever been acquitted of criminal charges?   Yes ___ No ___
    Have you ever been convicted of any crime other than a traffic
    violation?   Yes ___ No ___
    Have you ever been committed to an institution for mental health? Yes ___ No ___

    If so, how did you get out? _____

14. How would you describe your health?
    ___ Excellent ___ Good ___ Mediocre ___ Living on Borrowed Time

15. Name of Parent, Legal Guardian, or member of Opposite Sex with Whom You Reside:

    _____

    Relationship with above (check one): ___ Marital ___ Meaningful ___ Purely Casual

16. Parents
    Father's Name _____

    Occupation _____ Business Phone _____

    Annual Income _____ Liquid Assets _____

    Highest Level of School Attended: ___ Grade School ___ Junior High ___ High School
                                      ___ College (2 years) ___ College (4 years)

    Mother's Name _____

    Occupation _____ Business Phone _____

    Annual Income _____ Liquid Assets _____

    Your parents' first child was born how many months after their marriage?

    0–3 ___ 4–6 ___ 6–9 ___ 9 or more ___ Never ___

    Highest Level of School Attended: ___ Grade School ___ Junior High ___ High School
                                      ___ College (2 years)

17. Do you have any relatives who went to Mount Merry? No ___ Yes ___
    Won't Admit it ___

    If yes, how many years attended (if indeed they ever left)? _____
    Graduated? Yes ___ No ___

18. Please list the other colleges to which you are applying for admission, including any you
    consider a "safety school."

19. How did you first hear of Mount Merry?
    ___ Relative ___ College counselor at high school ___ Advertisement on matchbook
    ___ Bathroom wall

20. Which subjects do you think will most interest you in college, if any?

21. Which do you expect to dislike? _____

22. Would you be willing to take a history course?   ___Yes ___ No

23. Please list all the awards, prizes, honors, or elected offices you have won: _____

24. Have you pursued any of the following extracurricular activities in your school career?

    Would you be interested in pursuing them at Mount Merry?

    Newspaper ___   Computer Club ___   Boys ___   Girls ___   Marching Band ___

    Radio Club ___   Student Government ___   Eating ___   Dieting ___   Religion ___

    Glee Club ___   Dance ___   Reading ___

25. Are you interested in sports? Yes ___   No ___

26. Compared to other students in your school who are applying to selective colleges, how would you compare yourself in terms of skills or potential?

No basis		Below Average	Average	Good	Hopeless
	Creative, original thought				
	Motivation				
	Ability to stay awake				
	Intellectual ability				
	Written expression of ideas, if any				
	Class discussion				
	Effective class discussion				
	Disciplined work habits				
	Disciplined grooming habits				
	Potential for growth				
	Chances for growth				
	Summary evaluation				

27. Please list any hobbies or cultural pursuits you enjoy besides whittling, checkers, or weaving potholders:

_____

Essay Questions

The following essay questions are our way of getting to know YOU, the potential Mount Merry student. Please feel free to use additional paper of the same size and color or enclose samples of your work that you feel will tell us more about you as an individual. The Admissions Office is eager to receive tapes, 35mm slides, published creative work, cakes (especialy chocolate), sweaters (women's size 38), or any other supporting material.

1. Describe your most significant educational experience(s), physical or intellectual. Graphic detail is encouraged.

2. Why do you think Mount Merry might be an appropriate place to begin or end your education:

3. If there is some other question you wish we had asked? Please ask it now and answer it here.

RECOMMENDATION FORM

_____ has applied for admission to Mount Merry College. (You may know him or her as _____). If you know the student, please answer the following questions. The Admissions Office values your candid assessments and pledges to keep your comments confidential unless they're so juicy that she can't resist circulating them.

1. How long have you known the candidate?

2. In what capacity have you known the student?

   Pupil ___   Babysitter ___   Teacher's Pet ___
   Teacher ___   Date ___   Child or Blood Relative ___

3. What are the first words that come to your mind in describing the candidate?

   Capable ___   Enthusiastic ___   Rich ___   Gullible ___   "Nice" ___
   Intelligent ___ Loud ___   Easy ___   Obnoxious ___ Dumb ___

4. How would you rate the candidate's ability to succeed in college?

   7-to-1 ___   3-to-5 Against ___   Even Money ___   Long Shot ___

5. If the candidate is applying to transfer to Mount Merry, is he or she eligible to return to your institution, or do you want to get rid of him or her for good?

6. Has the candidate been subject to disciplinary action while at your school? If so, what was the offense? Please describe the punishment in explicit detail.

7. Check any special problems that would prevent the candidate from successful adjustment to college life.

   Laziness ___ Inability to add ___ Terminal acne ___ Inability to read ___
   Poverty ___ Irritating laugh ___ Flatulence ___ Startling resemblance to a baboon ___

   Please complete the following essay questions.

8. You and the candidate are shipwrecked on a desert island. Please give your reaction, the candidate's reaction, and to what lengths you would go to escape, if necessary.

9. Please use the space below to write a summary of the candidate including any relevant information, observation, and dirt.

10. This report on the candidate is based upon:

    Personal observation ___   Contact with candidate ___

    Records ___   Physical contact with candidate ___

    Teacher's comments ___

    Other counselor's private observations ___   Hearsay ___

    Information and remuneration supplied by candidate ___

11. How would you recommend this student for college?

    Recommended without hesitation ___ Recommended with reservations ___ Don't care ___

12. Is there any other student at your school you'd rather see admitted to Mount Merry?